ENEMY OF THE PEOPLE

ENEMY

OF THE

PEOPLE

Trump's War on the Press,
the New McCarthyism,
and the Threat
to American Democracy

MARVIN KALB

BROOKINGS INSTITUTION PRESS
Washington, D.C.

The Brookings Institution is a private nonprofit organization
devoted to research, education, and publication on important
issues of domestic and foreign policy. Its principal purpose is to
bring the highest quality independent research and analysis to
bear on current and emerging policy problems. Interpretations
or conclusions in Brookings publications should be understood
to be solely those of the authors.

Library of Congress Cataloging-in-Publication data are available.
ISBN 978-0-8157-3530-4 (cloth : alk. paper)
ISBN 978-0-8157-3531-1 (ebook)

9 8 7 6 5 4 3 2 1

Composition by Elliott Beard

Contents

Acknowledgments

I OWE THE IDEA for this book to the keen imagination of Bill Finan, director of the Brookings Institution Press. He sensed my concern for the future of a free press in America and proposed a book dedicated to the importance of a free press in a free society. In no way was the press ever to be considered an "enemy of the people." Quite the contrary! I am grateful to Bill and his dedicated staff—Yelba Quinn, Elliott Beard, Marjorie Pannell, John Felton, Steven Roman, Kristen Harrison, and C. J. Purdy—for making the passage from idea to book so smooth.

From the beginning of this effort, I have been encouraged by Jon Sawyer, executive director of the remarkable Pulitzer Center, where I have served as senior adviser. Kem Sawyer always sparked ideas while offering editorial direction. Both Sawyers provided a helping hand whenever they sensed I needed one. Nathalie Applewhite, Ann Peters, Jeff Bartholet, Tom Hundley, Karen Oliver, Jeff Barrus, Jin Ding, Steve Sapienza, and all the Fellows at the center were fabulously helpful and created a warm, friendly environment.

Next door, the Brookings Institution was a second home, where I was surrounded by friends loaded with intellectual stimulation. Led by the redoubtable John Allen, a former four-star Marine general, now president of the institution, Brookings always sought to make things better, and it often did.

Mike Freedman, the executive producer of *The Kalb Report*, a public affairs radio and television program now in its twenty-fifth year at the National Press Club, has always been a right arm for me, but, with this book, more so than ever. He provided ideas, energy, and encouragement until the writing was finally done. And then he did more.

Several friends put up with my questions and also served as sources of invaluable editorial guidance. Among them I must mention Andrew Glass, Garrett Mitchell, Walter Reich, and Stephen Hess. Many others helped too, but they led the parade.

As always, my incomparable brother, Bernard, read and edited every page, always encouraging, always dedicated to better journalism.

My daughters, Deborah and Judith, were unbelievably loving and supportive. The same for my sons-in-law, Alex Ogden and David Levitt. My grandchildren, Aaron and Eloise, are the emotional spark plugs of my life. I want them to inherit a better world, and that is not now certain.

Finally, with this book, even more than with the earlier ones, my wife, Madeleine, was the initial inspiration, and as the research and writing proceeded, she was always there with additional encouragement—and it was often needed during this project. Thank you, and bless you for never letting me forget that a free press, unafraid of official pressure or disparagement, is essential to the functioning of a free country. With a free press, we have the foundation of our democracy. Without it, we have. . . .

Preface

FOR THE LONGEST TIME, I did not take Donald Trump seriously; and when I did, finally, it was too late—he was already president of the United States, arguably the most powerful politician in the world.

When Trump launched his campaign for the presidency in June 2015, he was seen by many, me included, as a comic character, a real estate huckster who enjoyed life on the society pages of the New York tabloids, one divorce or scandal after another, jumping into the presidential run, as sixteen others already had, more for the fun of it, for the endless pursuit of personal glory, than for the opportunity to lead a great nation in a perilous time. With a canny mix of outrageous, off-the-cuff, anti-establishment, populist, seemingly senseless attacks on people, policy, and tradition and a clever exploitation of cable television news, he quickly rose to become the center of news coverage and conversation, conveying an impression of political strength, durability, and pizzazz. One sector of the

American electorate had been yearning for someone new and magically authentic, and Trump, with his catchy slogan— "Make America Great Again"—caught their eye and began filling their basket of expectations.

After a few months, one by one, his Republican opponents began dropping out of the race. They could not attract enough of the television coverage that Trump had successfully dominated with his wild, unorthodox eruptions. Without the coverage, they were soon without money. Donors looked elsewhere. By the summer of 2016 there was no one left in the once crowded field of GOP hopefuls except the jokester from Fifth Avenue. Trump had stumped the political world: he "won" most of the televised debates and an unusual number of primary elections. He might have started out as the unlikeliest of candidates, but, in July 2016, at the Republican National Convention, as TV pundits shook their heads in utter bewilderment and supporters dizzily screamed "Lock her up!"—referring to political opponent Hillary Clinton—Trump was officially crowned the GOP presidential nominee.

At the time, like many others, I watched Trump's remarkable rise as a major political force in American life, but, because I assumed that in the end Clinton, the Democratic frontrunner, would win the November election, I was not alarmed. I was troubled, of course, deeply disturbed that one of America's two major parties could settle on a candidate so clearly unprepared and unsuited to be president. I winced whenever I heard Trump demean judges and humiliate journalists, especially one with an obvious physical impairment; raise questions about the need for alliances such as NATO or trade agreements such as NAFTA; champion an "America First" domestic and foreign policy; question the government's role in providing affordable health care; and challenge environmental policies that have helped keep air and water clean and safe. He was certainly not my candidate—not because of his policy positions as a Republican (I had voted for many of those) but because he was Trump. Most especially, I suppose, because of the many years I spent covering the totalitarian excesses of the Soviet Union, I was upset that a presidential candidate would consistently undermine the values of a free press, which, for me, represented the heart and soul of a vibrant democracy.

But again, like so many others, I cushioned my concerns about Trump in the comfortable conviction that even though he was a very troubling prospect, Clinton would win the election and he would return to Trump Tower in New York, his tail between his legs.

Underappreciated at the time by both the U.S. government and the usually alert press corps was a considerable Russian effort to undermine the American electoral system, in the process doing the unimaginable in U.S.-Russian relations to this point: actively supporting one candidate, Trump, while undercutting the other, Clinton. Whether Russian help was decisive in Trump's ultimate victory might never be known definitively. Or whether the true explanation for Trump's unexpected victory lay in former FBI director James Comey's startling and unprecedented last-minute intrusions into the political process, which obviously undercut Clinton's prospects. Or whether it was Julian Assange's WikiLeaks, disgorging thousands of damaging emails about Clinton and her staff at key moments of the campaign—emails he reportedly obtained from the Russians by way of clever cutouts. Or whether, in the final analysis, the culprit was Clinton herself, unable, even with the winning hand she was dealt, to bring home the win.

For the moment, no matter the range of options, the big day, November 8, 2016, will inspire (in many ways, already has inspired) weighty analyses of Trump's legal coup of the Republican Party and the American political system. No one who attended an election night party, either Democratic or Republican, will ever forget the pro-Clinton elation, shown live on television, during the 8 to 9 p.m. hour (Eastern time), the uncertainty emerging in the 9 to 10 p.m. hour, the tipping of the electoral scales in the 10 to 11 p.m. hour, and then, finally, the pro-Trump ecstasy as the clock struck the midnight hour. The final votes from the key states of Wisconsin, Michigan, and Pennsylvania confirming his historic triumph were broadcast to the nation in the early morning hours.

I grasped the fact that Trump had won by the time I stumbled into bed that morning, but later that day and for much of the next few weeks, I could not quite accept the fact as fact. I found myself fighting the fact, waiting for a surprise of some sort to change the result of the election—a large box of chocolates, for example, in the shape of uncounted Clinton votes from Pittsburgh that would have miraculously swung Pennsylvania and the election to Clinton; or an unexpected announcement from GOP headquarters in Washington, D.C., that Trump really didn't want to be president, that he ran for no reason other than to prove to himself and the world that he could win; or a Kremlin admission of culpability that would have obliged the Supreme Court to call for a new election; anything but the fact, the unavoidability of which was slowly dawning on me, that Trump had won, fair and square (sort of), and would, on January 20, 2017, be officially sworn into office as the 45th president of the United States.

As I adjusted to this fact during the interregnum between Election Day and Inauguration Day (it took a lot of adjusting, even on such small things as linking the word "President" to the name "Trump," and then uttering them together as "President Trump"), I received an invitation from the Cosmos Club in Washington, D.C., to deliver a speech on February 16, 2017, about journalism's role in the history of American politics. Everyone seemed interested in Trump's often fiery criticism of the press and the controversial way cable television news had covered the campaign. For example, it was obvious that Trump had received far more free TV time than had any of the other candidates, including Clinton, during the long election cycle. How come? It was equally obvious that he also had received more space in newspapers. Again, how come?

I accepted the invitation, largely because I was fascinated by Trump's attitude toward the press. Was it simply an updating of Richard Nixon's antagonism toward the press? I knew that Nixon had ordered certain reporters, me included, to be wiretapped, their offices broken into and ransacked, and their tax returns arbitrarily audited; some, including me, were even placed on a frighteningly labeled "enemies list." Or was Trump's hostility toward the press something more menacing, going well beyond the traditional GOP playbook, which categorized most reporters as probable "enemies," into a new world of angry governmental crackdown, where a reporter's First Amendment guarantees of "freedom of the press" would be weakened and possibly even withdrawn? I wondered whether Trump suffered from an odd love-hate relationship with the press, yearning for its approval while at the same time despising and distrusting its power and influence. I wanted to learn more about Trump, and in the time needed to research and write a speech, I could learn a good deal about whether my earlier concerns about him were indeed justified. The speech in quick order became the first step toward writing this book, though I didn't know it at the time.

During his presidential campaign, Trump had clearly declared war on the press. His criticism was ugly, uninformed, and relentless. As someone who had spent six decades in the news business, either as a reporter or as a teacher, I found his descriptions of the press to be profoundly disturbing in their ignorance of history and potential for damage. Reporters were, in Trump's view, a "disgrace," dispensing "false, horrible, made-up news." They composed an "opposition party," a totally absurd idea but appealing to his conservative base, who seemed to enjoy attacking the press as much as a foreign enemy. Trump would often take time from his rambling campaign monologues to point to the reporters, producers, cameramen, and photographers, some by name but all kept behind roped barriers in the rear of a crowded auditorium or airport hangar, and declare them to be "dishonest people" who trafficked in "fake news." Predictably the reporters would be booed and hissed, the environment often edging toward overt hostility, even violence in some cases. A number of women reporters later admitted they were sometimes afraid to cover a Trump rally.

Trump was always, as journalists would say, "good copy," and he could count on extensive coverage. The television-watching public apparently loved it. Fox cable news covered Trump as if he were a political rock star; CNN and MSNBC, much the same. Trump, because of his wacky but eye-catching campaign, was a money-making machine for the news industry, a profit center at a time when it was in chronic financial need. Trump helped cable news, and cable news helped Trump win the election.

But as I started to write the speech, I faced an immediate problem, both personal and professional, defined in broad terms as a journalist's responsibilities when covering a story about which he had strong opinions. Would I be the same objective journalist I had tried to be for so many years, balancing the good and the bad, avoiding personal judgments, depending on fact, not opinion? Or could I, after all these years, drop my usual dedication to objective journalism and, for probably the first time in my professional life, tell the public what I truly felt about Trump and his approach to the press?

At this stage of my life (88 and counting) and at this delicate moment in American history (Trump's "Oh, my God!" election), I decided that I owed it as much to myself as to the public to pull back the green curtain of journalistic ethics behind which I had functioned for so many years and reveal, as honestly as possible, what I felt and feared about Trump's move into the White House. I was under no illusion that what I felt and feared about Trump was of any importance to anyone beyond my immediate family and circle of close friends, but it was still not an easy call. I also bemused myself into thinking the speech, when finally written and delivered, would go no further than the elegant halls of the Cosmos Club. I was wrong, and Trump, unwittingly, was the reason.

If Trump had been a genuine conservative, steeped in "born-again" religious beliefs and traditional GOP values, I might have been a political critic, but not one who, worried about the sudden weakening of American democracy, felt the need to rush to the rhetorical ramparts in defense of freedom. I would wait for the next election. I would return to writing my memoir, a promise I had made to my grandchildren. I would watch as America not only survived Trump but—who knows?—maybe even in some small ways thrived, as it always had in the past. In any case, all would be well in "this best of all possible worlds."

Except Trump has never been such a conservative. He was, depending on circumstance, all over the political map. He was once a Democrat who favored a woman's right to abortion and much else. He contributed to both political parties, later confessing it was primarily to purchase access. He supported

Hillary Clinton's run for the Senate. He was, in all, a reckless gambler, for whom a Sunday church service was about as foreign an experience as going to the opera or reading a good book.

Now, for reasons having more to do with political expediency than personal conviction, Trump has transformed himself into a Republican and a self-proclaimed populist, veering toward an unusual form of political authoritarianism completely antithetical to the norms of American democracy. He has personalized the presidency, converting the White House into an extension of his family business. He acts as if he considers the attorney general to be his personal lawyer and the rest of the government to be his fiefdom, obliged to do his bidding. He seems not to understand the checks and balances so essential to American governance. He thinks everything begins and ends with him. If unchecked, his personal style of governance, which after a while might be accepted as the norm in American politics, will undoubtedly dilute our democracy.

Since Trump clearly believes he is God's gift to America, he erupts with a special fury whenever he reads, or is told about, stories he regards as unfairly negative. Instinctive authoritarians like Trump believe they are entitled to a good press. When coverage, on TV and in print, becomes relentlessly negative, as it often has been for Trump, he feels he must find an enemy, a handy scapegoat. Who better than the press?

But it is not just the need for a scapegoat that inspires Trump's war on the press; it is also part of a cold, calculating strategy. If Trump can humiliate reporters, demonize them as peddlers of "fake news," and undercut their attachment to the rights and freedoms guaranteed in the First Amendment to the Constitution, then he can capitalize on the slow but undeniable erosion of popular trust and confidence in the American press seen in recent decades. Fewer Americans now believe in fact-based news; they'd rather trust the "news" coming from sympathetic outlets—Fox for the conservatives, MSNBC for the liberals. By attacking the press, Trump deepens this popular distrust, thereby weakening the ability of serious news organizations, such as the *New York Times* and the *Washington Post*, to inform the public.

CBS's Lesley Stahl told an interviewer at the Deadline Club in May 2018 that she once asked Trump why he kept attacking the press. His answer, according to Stahl: "I do it to discredit you all, and demean you all, so that when you write negative stories about me, no one will believe you."

A purely hypothetical example: if the *Times* reported that it was snowing but Trump argued that it was warm and sunny, claiming the *Times* report was another example of "fake news," then any number of his supporters, encouraged not to trust the "liberal" press, might choose to argue that, yes, indeed, it was sunny, even as they reached for their boots. A recent poll suggests that Trump may be winning this rhetorical struggle for "truth." It points out that since Trump has begun to attach the "fake news" label to any story critical of him or his policies, 62 percent of the American people have confessed to having less "trust" in the truthfulness of the media (75 percent, if Republican; 50 percent, if Democrat). In this shifting environment, a White House emphasis on "alternative facts," a fanciful concoction created by White House aide Kellyanne Conway, might swing a point or two in a national poll, and this small change might then encourage a vote or two in Congress to pass a controversial piece of legislation. Facts might no longer be the measure of good journalism or good governance.

At this point, I felt I had marshaled enough of the facts, judgments, and opinions about Trump's war on the press to write my speech, which I did a few days before its dinnertime delivery on February 16, 2017.

But late that afternoon, Trump unintentionally forced me to rewrite the opening of my speech. A few of my friends alerted me to the fact that, later that night, Trump was going to add a stinging new acid to his ritual assault on the press. In tweet form, he was going to accuse the press of being "the enemy of the American people." I had thought, up to that moment, that Trump had reached the outer limits of tolerable criticism of the American press, but with this tweet, he crossed a line. He was now displaying a scary un-Americanism, a kind of authoritarianism foreign to the American political and cultural experience. Wittingly or not, he was embracing a slogan of fear and hate associated with the worst tyrants of the twentieth century—Stalin, Hitler, and Mao. I wondered, was Trump aware of this association? No, I thought.

With rewrite in hand, aware that I was entering a new sphere of editorial commentary, at least for me, I proceeded to the Cosmos Club, where I found the renovated main ballroom filled with people eager to hear a talk about Trump's war on the press. In the audience was my colleague, Mike Freedman. He was, years ago, general manager of CBS Radio News, and now, in his still-busy day, he works two jobs: as senior vice president of the University of Maryland University College and executive producer of *The Kalb Report*, a public affairs radio and television program I have been hosting at the National Press Club for the past 24 years. Mike was reassuringly positive in his reaction to my speech—in fact, enthusiastically so. He suggested I deliver a speech with the same message at the National Press Club, where he hoped it would be carried live on its website and then transmitted to similar clubs and journalism schools around the country. Mike wanted to create a buzz, a journalistic firewall to counter Trump's angry assault on the American press. Like many journalists, Mike was distressed by Trump's victory—first, that Trump was now president of the country Mike so loved, and second, that Trump could go so far as to accuse the press of being the "enemy of the American people."

If Mike, at that moment, could have persuaded a Walter Cronkite or an Edward R. Murrow to defend the press against Trump's unwarranted assault, he would surely have turned to them. Mike felt the country needed a journalist who would speak up for the press now, someone who either had or had once had a national following on television. Having heard my speech, knowing of my journalistic and academic background, Mike concluded that he had found his spokesman. "Whaddayasay?" he asked, a trace of urgency in his voice. I was flattered, of course, but certain that Mike needed someone much younger, better known, hooked into social media, and decidedly political. I failed on all counts, but Mike was not persuaded. "Tell the National Press Club what you have just told the Cosmos Club," he said, "and the word will spread." I assured Mike I would think about his proposal and call him the next morning, and we would talk. On the drive home, I began to change my mind. Even if I were far from the ideal spokesman, I could still do my part, modest though it be, and maybe others, more prominent, better connected, would follow. I also thought about Russian journalists who could not speak truth to power but would leap at such a chance. The moment I got home, I called Mike. "Let's give it a shot," I said. "It is certainly worth the effort." The effort was still not this book, not in my mind anyway, but it was another step in my decision to write it.

Within a few days, Mike, who is a work addict, had a date: March 29, 2017. He had a very large room—the Edward R. Murrow Room. (I thought about Murrow's defense of a free press in his momentous battle with Senator Joe McCarthy in the early 1950s.) Mike also had a camera crew and the assurance of the National Press Club that its website would carry the speech. And maybe C-SPAN would cover it.

The major difference between the two speeches was that I spent more time in the Press Club version emphasizing the values of a free press, notwithstanding Trump's sustained criticism of "fake news." No matter the erosion of popular support, the blistering criticism of many political conservatives, the continuing financial pressures on most media outlets, leading to budgetary and bureau cuts, the shrinkage of coverage at home and abroad, there was still in America a free and vibrant press, inspired by two great newspapers, and by the work of brave young reporters in covering wars, terrorist attacks, famine, disease, and immigration upheavals all over the world. My point was that we make the mistake of taking the everyday miracle of a free press for granted. It remains a precious gift—in my mind, the foundation of our democracy—and it should be nurtured, supported, and honored.

As summer slipped into fall, Mike and I prepared for the next edition of *The Kalb Report*, set for October 16, 2017. We spent many hours reminiscing about the central thesis of the two speeches, wondering not whether but how the Trump saga could be woven into the broadcast. Since I had spent so much time extolling the virtues of the *New York Times* and the *Washington Post*, especially in their trailblazing coverage of Trump's attacks on the rule of law and the freedom of the press, Mike and I both came up with the same idea at roughly the same time—let's try to get the two top editors of the newspapers to be our guests: Dean Baquet, executive editor of the *Times*, and Martin Baron, executive editor of the *Post*. They had been colleagues at different times in their careers, and both had been our guests in earlier broadcasts, but separately. We knew they were fiercely competitive and had never appeared together on the same program. The odds were against us, but I sent a welcoming invitation to both, using the same email and, following the etiquette of the alphabet, placing Baquet before Baron in the salutation but Marty before Dean in the "Dear . . ." greeting. Baron answered first—"yes," he accepted—and Baquet second—"yes," he too accepted. We had the makings of an important broadcast. C-SPAN agreed, and carried it live.

It was an exciting broadcast. Both denied they were working together to topple Trump from power, but took evident pride in their reporting of Trump's unorthodox presidency. "We are not at war with the president," Baron insisted; "we're at work, doing our job." Baquet said that when he was Washington bureau chief during the Obama years, he never once met the president, and that was the way he wanted it. Distance between the press and the president was his preferred policy. Baron acknowledged that Trump's frequent attacks on the press had darkened the relationship between the press and the president, adding to the pressures on the press, but had not changed the press's basic responsibility—to cover the news "without fear or favor." Like Baquet, he was happy to keep the president, any president, as far away from his reporters as possible.

I had never used the broadcast to express an editorial opinion. Questions, please, no opinions. But on this broadcast, for the first time, I added a brief commentary to the standard conclusion. As Baron and Baquet watched, I said things I had probably never before uttered in public—and I probably never would have, if I had not been provoked by Trump's "enemy of the people" attack on the press:

"In my career, I spent a lot of time covering the Soviet Union," I began. "It was governed by communists. They had little taste or understanding of personal freedom, much less press freedom. Everything was determined by the *vozhd*, the Russian word for a strong leader who ran everything from the Kremlin, who thought he knew more than anyone else. As a result, everyone, from doctors to reporters, had to stand up and salute—never to rock the boat, never to be critical of him or his policies.

"I did not like that arbitrary style of governance then, and I don't like it now. What I have learned over the years—and many have accumulated—is that only a free press can truly protect us from authoritarian government. Only a free press can insure a continuation of a vibrant democracy. The two are inseparable.

"If a political leader finds it to his advantage to attack a free press, to humiliate it, to disparage it, he is really attacking democracy at its core, and that has no place in this country." I paused to let the thought sink in. Then, mindful of the fact that I was speaking at the National Press Club and hoping to absolve it of any responsibility for what I said, I added, perhaps unnecessarily, "at least, that is my view."

No one should have had any trouble linking my criticism of a "political leader" to Trump. He was my target. Many in the ballroom rushed to the platform when the program ended and complimented the two editors and me for an enlightening broadcast. Quite a few lingered to express their agreement with my commentary. Even though I always felt Mike exaggerated the impact of my message—he remains the eternal optimist, bless him—I was delighted that many people were at least hearing it.

A few days later, I received an enticing email from William (Bill) Finan, soon to be named director of the Brookings Institution Press. He had attended my NPC interview with Baquet and Baron. He wrote that he was impressed by the message in my concluding commentary—the importance of a free press in sustaining and possibly strengthening democratic values— and wondered whether I would consider doing a book on this theme. I suggested in a return email that we meet the following week and discuss it—a sensible way, I thought, of avoiding a snap decision. I was still busy with book promotion, having only recently enjoyed the publication of *The Year I Was Peter the Great—1956: Khrushchev, Stalin's Ghost, and a Young American in Russia*, the first in a projected three-volume memoir, and I was already giving serious thought to volume two. Did I want to be distracted by Trump's war on the press?

Yes, I did, I concluded, and there were two reasons, both related to Trump's accession to the presidency. A book would be a natural successor to my speeches and commentaries, another way of continuing to spread the word about Trump's dangerous attacks on a free press and the rule of law, on the essence of American democracy. And if I was truly serious about spreading the word, then I had to seize this moment—and write. The word was my weapon of persuasion, and the time was now. If Trump wanted to fight for his vision of America, then I had no option but to fight for mine.

When Bill and I met, the project was launched. Bill wanted a short book—40,000 to 50,000 words. He urged a tight deadline and rapid publication. I agreed.

By the time I left Bill's office, I had a possible title for the book already in mind. If Trump could raise the grotesquely unfair charge of the American press being the "enemy of the people," then I could justifiably turn the phrase on him. It was not, in my judgment, the press that was the "enemy of the people." It was Trump.

Chevy Chase, Maryland
June 9, 2018

ENEMY OF THE PEOPLE

ONE

Crossing a Flashing Red Line

ON FEBRUARY 17, 2017, newly inaugurated President Donald J. Trump tweeted:

> The FAKE NEWS media (failing @nytimes, @NBCNews, @ABC, @CBS, @CNN) is not my enemy, it is the enemy of the American People!

A few days later he unleashed another tweet:

> I called the fake news the 'enemy of the people' because they have no sources—they just make it up.

Many Americans were surprised, some even shocked. Reporters, of course, could not believe what they were reading. Like most Americans, they had been raised on First Amendment assurances of "freedom of the press." For the president, this might have been nothing more than a frightening bark

1

with no bite intended. But by using that phrase, "enemy of the people," the president had crossed a flashing red line.

Reading the tweet, I was left wondering: did he not realize that only dictators, detached from democratic norms and values, would use such a phrase?

And yet, that was what he had tweeted—and much more. The press, he said, was a "disgrace . . . false, horrible, fake reporting." It was "out of control . . . fantastic." Reporters were "the most dishonest people." Their coverage was an "outrage." The *New York Times* was a "failing" newspaper; CNN, "terrible" with "lousy ratings compared to Fox"; *BuzzFeed*, "garbage." Trump even questioned the press's patriotism. "I really don't think they like our country," he said, adding the press was a "stain on America."

On occasion, he personalized his critique of the media, calling NBC's Chuck Todd a "sleeping son of a bitch" and the *Times*'s Maggie Haberman a "Hillary flunky, who knows nothing about me and is not given access." (Haberman has in fact interviewed Trump quite a few times.)

A White House adviser, when questioned by reporters, stuck to the party line. "Yes," he stressed, "that is exactly what the president means: the press is the 'enemy of the people.'"

Yet a few days later, on February 22, during a speech before the Conservative Political Action Committee (CPAC), Trump tried to refine his attack on the press, explaining his target was really "fake news," not the "press" as such. "The dishonest media did not explain," he said, as CPAC members stood and cheered, "that I called the fake news the enemy of the people— the fake news. They dropped off the word 'fake.' And all of a sudden the story became, 'the media is the enemy.' They take the word 'fake' out." His audience loudly applauded, as Trump continued, "Now I'm saying, 'oh, no, this is no good.' But that's the way they are. So I'm not against the media. I'm not against the press. . . . I am only against the fake news media or press— fake, fake. They have to leave that word [in]." While acknowledging there were "some great reporters around, honest as the day is long," probably having Fox cable news in mind, Trump left the clear impression that in his mind the "press" was divided into two broad categories: those who are friends and those who are foes. The friends praise him regularly; the foes, dealing in "fake news," criticize him. Since by his own definition most of the press was critical of him and his administration, they were to be considered foes, or "enemies of the people," "doing a tremendous disservice to our country and to our people." And they were to be attacked.

Soon the president's artificial distinction between friend and foe vanished.

From George Washington to . . . Donald Trump?

With an odd mix of pride and defiance, Donald Trump, the unlikeliest of presidents in a line dating back to George Washington, has set his own marker on American history. Rather than uphold the First Amendment guarantee of freedom of the press, as had all of his predecessors, both Republican and Democratic (except perhaps for John Adams with the Alien and Sedition Acts and Richard Nixon with his "enemies list"), he has chosen to attack the press as an "enemy of the people," saying on more than one occasion that the First Amendment provides "too much protection" for the press. He has also threatened to "open up the libel laws," which he called a "sham and a disgrace," though this is beyond his authority, rooted as libel laws are in state, not federal, law. He urged James Comey, at the time his FBI director, later a political enemy, to start more "leak" investigations and put more reporters in prison for publishing classified information. Indeed, his attorney general, Jeff Sessions, hoping to score a few points with his boss, boasted that the Justice Department was now conducting twenty-seven "leak" investigations, three times as many as the Obama administration, which itself had launched a record number.

As Trump might add in one of his now-famous tweets, "SAD!"

Trump seems to derive a special pleasure from smashing existing protocol, attempting to prove to one and all that he is an outsider who will "never lie" and will "always fight for the forgotten Americans." That he also has proved, even while in office, to be a congenital liar and far more absorbed with the pleasures and profits of corporate executives than with the needs of jobless workers seems not to disturb him or his so far loyal base.

According to the *Washington Post*'s Fact Checker, Trump made 3,001 "false or misleading claims" in his first 466 days as president, an average of six a day.[1] The *New York Times*, which never before used the word "lie" to describe a "false or misleading claim" by a sitting president, has now begun to use the word "lie" to describe a "false claim" by Trump. On one of his first days in office, Trump told a lie that he was to repeat many times—that the crowd at his inauguration was much larger than the crowd at Barack Obama's inauguration. He ordered his new press secretary, Sean Spicer, to exaggerate the size of the crowd at his first White House press briefing. The *Times* checked Trump's public statements and found that he told a "public lie" or a "falsehood" every day for the first forty days of his presidency and, since then, on "at least 74 of 113 days."[2] Editors determined that "lie" was an accurate if somewhat jarring word, and they have begun to use it when appropriate. But no matter his lying, his outrageous personal conduct, or his disruptive policy proclamations, his 30 to 40 percent support among Americans held firm well into 2018.

Trump, we can hope, is a once-in-a-lifetime experience, a real estate magnate who had never held political office, never served in the military (having received five deferments for college and a "bone spur"), and never demonstrated any serious interest in, or familiarity with, foreign or domestic policy. And yet he managed, in the totally bizarre presidential race of 2016, to diminish and demolish sixteen other GOP candidates and then, against the best Las Vegas odds, upset his Democratic opponent, Hillary Clinton, leaving the experts in politics and journalism shaking their heads in disbelief. One big question was whether Russian interference in the 2016 election might have helped swing it in Trump's direction. By the end of the campaign, Russians left little doubt they detested Clinton and by implication favored Trump, but definitive proof of their role awaited the result of ongoing investigations. James Clapper, the former director of national intelligence, while promoting a book, offered his opinion, based, as he said, on "logic and credulity," that the Russians "actually turned it" in Trump's direction, but not even he, as a top intelligence analyst, could be certain.

Throughout his career as a real estate huckster, Trump has always been intrigued with the media; notably, he cherished his anchor role on NBC's *The Apprentice*. "You're fired!" he enjoyed shouting. Television's potential for self-aggrandizement fascinated Trump. It converted him into a national figure. Loving all publicity, good or bad, savoring an article or photo of himself like a connoisseur of good wine, boasting about how many times he made the cover of *Time*, Trump has always been happiest when he is center-stage—whether on TV or in headlines. Some presidents spend many lonely hours studying briefing books on arms control, climate change, and similar weighty topics. Trump reportedly spends barely an hour, if that, on briefing books each day and as many as four to eight hours a day watching cable television, notably his favorite show: *Fox and Friends*. For him, television is a constant source of ego gratification, the fount of all knowledge, even the basis for snap policy decisions.

Of course, Trump denies watching a lot of television. "People with fake sources—you know fake reporters, fake sources" made the accusation, he said. "But I don't get to watch much television, primarily because of documents. I'm reading documents a lot."[3] That would depend on the translation of "a lot."

Trump's senior staff at the White House understand that he likes to think of each day as a TV reality show in which he, the president, is shown conquering a policy dragon, looking like a strong leader, setting ratings records. Only then should the staff think about the next day's theme. According to an agreed-upon plan of diversion, an official, who is theoretically pledged never to leak secret information to the press, leaks the "secret information" that next week the president is going to announce a change in, say, the country's nuclear policy—one that would have the effect of creating chaos and confusion in every defense establishment around the world. The point is to hook the journalist on the next Trump adventure or misadventure, leaving him or her with little or no time to explore more deeply the current calamity. "Tune in," as a TV tactic, rivets the reporter to the future. That keeps the reporter guessing, and that is part of the plan. After a while, reporters realized what Trump was doing, but they could not do anything about it. As professionals, they still had the responsibility to cover that day's news—and ignoring Trump the president was not an option.

Still, after only a relatively brief time in office, there can be no doubt that he has changed the politics and culture of the country, introducing a style of governance utterly unfamiliar to the American experience. (Will we be able to return, post-Trump, to something more familiar?) His style could be called creeping authoritarianism mixed with galloping inefficiency, a narcissistic sun king model of personal rather than institutional, law-based power. He believes he stands at the pinnacle of the American dream and deserves the respect of the people and the personal honor afforded him by the office. No other person, no institution inside or outside the government, should challenge him. Congress, the courts, the law, the press, the talk shows—all ought to be there to help him govern, not to complicate his life with questions or dissent. Subordinates rule their fiefdoms only after swearing unwavering fealty to him and his vision. He, by his own reckoning, is a "genius," deserving his place in the sun. With all of his vulnerabilities, legal and moral, he still strides across a nation he might like, one day, to rebrand as "Trump."

All of this is why it is more than an academic exercise to ask questions relating to his distorted understanding of "freedom of the press": how did he come upon the phrase "enemy of the people," and what does it mean to him? And can American democracy survive if "freedom of the press" is systematically undercut and undervalued by the president and his minions?

After more than sixty years as a journalist, working at home and abroad, I have come to the conclusion that a free press and democracy are tightly intertwined, each sustaining the other. Lose one, and you lose the other. A free press guarantees a free society, a functioning and, one hopes, flourishing democracy. Therefore, when a president attacks the press as an "enemy of the people," he is doing more than delegitimizing, demeaning, and trivializing the so-called fourth branch of government. He is also attacking the very foundation of American democracy—and he must be challenged and either stopped or somehow persuaded to change his ways.

The press has become a crucially important yardstick for measuring whether a nation tilts toward democracy or away from it. I remember, as a young reporter in the 1950s, writing about ambitious colonels in Central America staging a coup and immediately seizing control of the radio station to broadcast the news that a new day has finally arrived and it's now best to sit back, listen, and obey the new junta. Obviously, radio as an instant messenger to the people was considered more important than control of the local constabulary.

Or, whenever I arrived in a new country, I would pay a quick visit to the nearest news kiosk, usually located on the other side of passport control. One look was enough to know a lot about the political complexion of the government: whether it was a democracy or an autocracy, whether the press was free or a servant of the state. Not just the headlines but also the size and placement of front-page photos—especially of leaders— would tell much about the politics of the country.

Or, during the Soviet period, talking to a *Pravda* or an *Izvestia* reporter, who would tell me that, in *Pravda* (the Russian word for "truth") there was no "truth," and in *Izvestia* (the Russian word for "news") there was no "news." There was only what the state, in the person of an editor acting on behalf of the Kremlin, wanted the reporter to tell the people, no more, no less. Lenin always said that the press was not a doorway to democracy but an instrument of political control. It served only a utilitarian end; it was not a romance.

After 1991, when the Soviet Union fell apart and communist constraints collapsed, Russians saw the dawning of a new democracy. It proved to be a false dawn, but for a time it was intoxicating. People enjoyed the freest press they had ever known. They spoke their minds. But when Vladimir Putin began to solidify his hold on power, he moved quickly against the television networks (the modern-day equivalent of the old radio stations) and then the newspapers, and Russia's brief experiment with freedom faded into history. Only a whimper of its memory can now be heard.

And the American press today, under Trump? Though still pressured by collapsing budgets, new technology, and greedy owners—and undermined by a president who labels it an "enemy of the people"—it remains a vigorous, free, and, most of the time, responsible press, fully capable of covering all aspects of an unprecedented presidency. Indeed, a look at American history strongly suggests that the press, along with the sanctity of the law, is the foundation of American democracy. When the press is attacked, so too is our democracy.

Enter Pat Caddell

So how did Trump, who rarely reads a book, come upon the phrase "enemy of the people"? He once explained his approach to book reading. "I'm an intuitive person," he said. "I read passages [of books]. I read areas. I'll read chapters." Or, more likely, nothing at all.

It has been said, perhaps in jest, that the last person who has Trump's ear is, for that moment, the most influential person in the country. While that may be true, it also seems that the future president continues to be influenced by a speech delivered years earlier by a brilliant, though angry, Democratic pollster, repeated in a *Breitbart* radio interview and then published on the *Breitbart* website. It was a speech delivered by Pat Caddell.

If, during the heat of the 2016 campaign, candidate Trump needed a reassuring pat on the back, he would turn, ironically, to the speeches or broadcasts of his new political buddy, Caddell, who four decades earlier had been a major force in propelling a little-known former governor of Georgia, Jimmy Carter, to become president of the United States in 1976. Caddell's message, in the 1976 campaign as well as in the 2016 campaign, was that the majority of Americans, 85 percent in his judgment, believed that the political and economic system was "rigged" against them, and a sweeping change, a "drain the swamp" revolution, was needed to right the wrongs so obvious to clear-thinking but forgotten Americans living in the heartland of the country. (Many of those on the East and West Coasts were described as satisfied with the existing system because it benefited them.)

One reason, argued Caddell, was that the American press had lost its connection to the people. It had become hopelessly "corrupt," refusing to run stories critical of the Washington establishment and was "in bed" with the political and economic elite. Worse, the network anchors and newspaper columnists themselves had become part of the elite, and they had to be made the target of an angry, outlier candidate, the candidate Caddell now saw in Trump.

The Caddell playbook contained the strands of the erratic populism soon to define the Trump presidency. It also echoed antimainstream media themes dating back to the Nixon administration, when Vice President Spiro Agnew branded the media as the "nattering nabobs of negativism" and the northeast corner of the country—the Boston-New York-Washington corridor—as a place of wild, incestuous liberalism. "We" ordinary Americans were recognizable and familiar; "they" were foreign and hostile, the we/they split defining a central theme in conservative campaign rhetoric to this day. Nixon claimed to represent the "silent majority" of Americans; Trump the "forgotten" Americans.

Though a Democrat who had earlier labored for Joe Biden, Jerry Brown, and Gary Hart, in addition to Carter, Caddell appealed to Trump, himself a former Democrat. Caddell was a regular contributor to Fox News. He was the subject of countless favorable articles on the conservative *Breitbart* website, which Trump read regularly, and he was heard often enough on *Breitbart* radio to become a good friend of Stephen Bannon, who had been *Breitbart*'s chief before becoming, for a time, Trump's ideological Darth Vader. (*Time*, in a cover story, called Bannon "The Great Manipulator," and NBC's *Saturday Night Live* showed him as a skeleton in a black cloak, dictating policy to a smaller, shriveled Trump.) Bannon had become a Caddell soulmate, sharing nuggets of wisdom, or nuttiness, about the state of the nation's press and politics. It was Caddell's notion of the press as the "enemy of the American people" that eventually found its way into Trump's mind.

On July 31, a notable Sunday in the 2016 campaign because it followed the official coronation of Trump as the GOP candidate for president, Caddell again appeared on the *Breitbart News Daily*, a radio program distributed by Sirius/XM Satellite radio. Host Alex Marlow reminded his listeners that Caddell was one of the very few pollsters who had correctly predicted Trump's emergence from the crowded GOP field to become the party's nominee. Marlow hoped that now the American people would see how "rigged" the system really was, how Hillary Clinton "lied through her teeth," how the Benghazi "victims" were being forgotten, and how "innocent Americans" were being "murdered by illegal aliens." To say, on reflection, that Marlow loaded his question with Trump's campaign rhetoric would be a modest understatement, but Caddell seized on the opportunity to trumpet his favorite criticism of the press.

"They are . . . they're making themselves, as I've said before, *the enemies of the American people*, and the American people don't think much of them now and won't think much of them," opined Caddell. "But you cannot let them get away with this, the way people like Romney and others roll over and take a beating, because their consultants want to make sure they preserve their relationships in Washington with the political media."[4]

Obviously pleased with Caddell's response, Marlow then went on to describe Caddell as "a Democratic pollster and a contributor to Breitbart, one of the most knowledgeable men in politics." Caddell added that he, Fox News, and the *Wall Street Journal* had all come up with "a lot of numbers and things" that proved that "the real message here" was that "if [Trump] can learn to hit big ground . . . and discipline himself, he is the man to beat in this election, not her [Clinton]. She ain't got anywhere to go in my opinion, unless Trump blows himself up." Most other pollsters reckoned at the time that Hillary Clinton would win easily.

It took no special insight to understand that Trump loved Caddell's projection, and he began to listen to the Democratic pollster more regularly on *Breitbart* and Fox News. Trump especially loved Caddell's praise of his campaign slogan "Make America Great Again," Caddell calling it "the greatest slogan of my lifetime." Bannon, already a friend and admirer of Caddell, pointed out to Trump that Caddell had been singing this same anti-elite, antimedia tune for years. In 2012 Caddell had delivered a speech based on an article he wrote for *Breitbart* called "The Audacity of Corruption," in which he ripped into the press for rupturing the "thin balance" between a "free democracy" and a privileged autocracy. Trust between the press and the public was rapidly evaporating, he said, posing a "fundamental danger" to the republic. Sixty percent of the American people, according to Gallup, trusted the press "not very much" or "not at all." "The press's job," stressed Caddell, "is to stand on the ramparts and protect the liberty and freedom of us all from . . . organized governmental power." But when the press "deserts those ramparts" and becomes "active participants" in the political process, telling you "who to vote for" and what is truth and what is not, then "they have made themselves a fundamental threat to the democracy, and, in my opinion, made themselves the enemy of the American people."[5]

Caddell, in 2012, had a nightmarish vision—that one day a frightening composite of George Wallace and Huey Long would run for president and claim, on the campaign trail, that the press was "biased" and "out to get me," and "this First Amendment stuff" had gone "too far and "we need to make [the press] serve the people." The press was losing its value to the people, hypothesized Caddell, and the people would soon lose their faith in the press. "Why do we need a First Amendment?" Caddell fancifully quoted the composite candidate as asking. Without a satisfactory answer, the pollster believed, the country would go into a "deep slide" toward authoritarianism.

Caddell stressed that "we desperately need a real free press," one that would tell the truth and reclaim the trust of the American people. Or else, "at the end of the day, somebody's going to say, 'Enough of this [democracy]!' And somebody will carry the day, and that'll be that." In other words, Caddell's deep-seated fear in 2012 was that an autocrat would rise to take advantage of a failing press and overturn American democracy. How he could reconcile his apparently genuine fear of a Wallace-Long autocrat with his amazing admiration for Trump never made much sense, but there it was. Four short years later, Caddell would be the inspiring wordsmith who pulled "enemy of the people" out of communist mothballs and put it in the contemporary employ of a Wallace-Long-type candidate from New York who had little to no respect for or knowledge of First Amendment guarantees of "freedom of the press," and who one day might himself conclude "enough of this" democracy stuff, and, as Caddell predicted, "that'll be that."

Bannon's "Alt-Right" Monstrosity

It was not Caddell alone who persuaded Trump that the press had become the "enemy of the people." A larger role was played by Bannon, who proudly referred to his *Breitbart* empire as the "platform of the alt-right," a controversial movement of right-wing, antiblack, anti-Semitic, anti-Muslim conservatives who felt their time had come because of their attachment to Trump's startling political emergence. Shortly after Caddell hammered his press-as-enemy slogan on the *Breitbart* masthead in July 2016, Bannon himself was recruited by candidate Trump—who was troubled by falling poll numbers—to inject more energy and new ideas into his faltering campaign. Bannon became the chief operating officer, and Kellyanne Conway, a veteran GOP pollster and strategist, became campaign manager. Trump seemed not in the least bothered by the fact that Conway had never before run a presidential campaign or that *Breitbart*, under Bannon's leadership, had been poisoning the political well with racist and white supremacist conspiracy theories. "I'll do whatever I can to win," Trump said, justifying his selections.

Bannon was a firebrand America Firster and populist who was at different times in a busy life a U.S. Navy officer, a vice president at Goldman Sachs, and a writer or producer of eighteen Hollywood movies—including such winners as *Destroying the Great Satan: The Rise of Islamic Fascism in America* and *The Chaos Experiment.* He served Trump's needs for only a year—four months on a victorious campaign, then eight months in a turbulent White House—before being banished into political exile for crossing Trump once too often, including by taking too much of the attention that Trump wanted for himself. It was a relatively brief political marriage. But during the time he stood at Trump's side, he was a significant force in White House deliberations.

Bannon represented what he considered big ideas, and many of them overlapped with Trump's. Those ideas that were very controversial, such as expelling illegal immigrants and restricting legal immigration, whenever possible, to white people, were sugarcoated with evasions intended to appeal to Trump's base. (Trump opened his campaign by referring to "Mexicans" as "rapists.") They both opposed trade pacts, such as the North American Free Trade Agreement (NAFTA), and they even had questions about NATO, which shocked many of America's traditional allies. Bannon, who had at one time hustled in Southeast Asia for big business deals, came to distrust China; he argued, for example, that one day Chinese aggression in the South China Sea would lead to a war with the United States. Both men favored rolling back regulations, or, as Bannon put it, the "deconstruction of the administrative state." The "deep state," as he later called it, was perceived as an enemy force composed of entrenched career bureaucrats—all liberals and Democrats in this fantasy—who were out to get Trump, to deny him the policy successes he had already earned and to sabotage his chances of future success.

On occasion, Bannon surprised even his White House colleagues, driven as he was by dark visions of an onrushing global apocalypse or imagining himself as a Russian revolutionary determined to uproot the old order and install a new one. Once, in conversation with a Russia scholar, he bluntly proclaimed, "I am a Leninist."

The scholar was stunned. "Leninist?" he asked. "What do you mean?"

Bannon replied, "Lenin wanted to destroy the state, and that's my goal too. I want to bring everything crashing down and destroy all of today's establishment."

Working in the White House, Bannon was in an excellent position to realize many of his "Leninist" dreams.

Manipulating the Media

Even though he was, in his latest incarnation, a media man, Bannon, like Caddell, was deeply suspicious of the mainstream press. He fully shared Trump's belief that most of the media had abandoned any pretense of objectivity during the 2016 campaign and openly sided with Hillary Clinton's bid for the presidency. Major newspapers, such as the *New York Times* and the *Washington Post,* not only ran long editorials favoring a Clinton triumph but, in Trump's view, underplayed Clinton's email problems while overplaying his own problems, of which there were many. In fact, Trump "owned" one of the most important media franchises, the Fox News channel. He appeared on it more than any other campaigning politician and received endlessly favorable coverage on it—and he attacked Fox competitors CNN and MSNBC for being "unfair" and refusing to give him a "fair" amount of air time, which was simply not true. On all three cable news channels, Trump was seen and heard almost anywhere at any time. He was covered not only as a presidential candidate but also as a TV rock star. He was, in a way, his own TV producer, deciding when and how he would appear, and he almost always got his way.

For example, on morning interview shows, Trump, rather than appear in person, would simply call Fox or another television news program and speak to the host on the phone. His photo would be shown, his voice heard, and his policies explained. That made life easier for Trump during a heavy campaign day. Normally the networks would have insisted that a candidate show up in person at the studio. I remember, when I hosted *Meet the Press* in the 1980s, that guests would have to appear in person or they would not have been welcomed on the program. But in 2016, for Trump, who seemed to make news even when he said nothing of substance, the networks changed their rule books. They were so eager to have Trump on air, they took him whenever he chose to call. He was their meal ticket during the campaign, and he remains so now that he is in office.

According to the respected *Tyndall Report,* the three big TV networks—ABC, CBS, and NBC—also twisted their rules to show as much of Trump as they could, all to his political advantage. Because Trump was so unusual a political character, he attracted eyeballs and boosted network ratings, and the three networks made a lot of money. They helped elect Trump in 2016 by giving him 1,144 minutes of free TV coverage compared to only 506 minutes for Clinton, more than double the time.[6]

One remarkable aspect of Trump's coverage was that he generated high ratings even when the news about him was decidedly negative. It didn't seem to matter. Many of his supporters distrusted the media so much they refused to believe critical reporting about him—and critical reporting merely reinforced their negative views of the media. Likewise, many of his critics were so tantalized by Trump's latest outrage that they, too, could not get enough of him. Even when his critics were disgusted by something Trump said or did, as in the *Access Hollywood* tape when he boasted that his "celebrity" allowed him to "grab" women "by the pussy," they still watched him, or read about him, and that has been a source of his continuing political strength. Experts have been waiting for his inevitable collapse; they are still waiting.

"Their Finger on the Scales"

Trump is a totally self-absorbed political phenomenon. Though once a Democrat who favored birth control and gun control, he now appeals to a solidly conservative base, including many other former Democrats who have veered to the right along with him. After his election, he could have extended an olive branch to the media, so instrumental were they in his victory. But instead, almost from day one of his presidency, Trump has declared war on the press—the "opposition party," as he repeatedly puts it, the "enemy of the people." He apparently believes the media has always been out to get him, and he is determined to fight back. That was what Roy Cohn, his mentor and counsel in New York, had always advised. Fight back, Cohn would say; never admit a mistake. Kellyanne Conway has a ready explanation, too (she always does), and, not surprisingly, it goes back to the 2016 campaign, when Trump, in her judgment (and his), was the most "vilified and attacked politician" ever, subject to horrible "negative coverage." The press, she argues, "suspended the objective standards of journalism," putting "their finger on the scales" for Clinton. They were "unfair," she says, using one of Trump's favorite words. Added a White House colleague, "I don't think he will ever be treated fairly. I don't think he ever was treated fairly."

Even now, in Trump's second year in office, Conway has not changed her tune. "It's incredible to watch people play armchair psychologist," she says, "outright ridiculing the president's physicality, his mental state, calling him names that you won't want your children to call people on a playground . . . and then all of a sudden feigning shock when he wants to fight back and defend himself."[7]

Bannon, characteristically, was even blunter in his criticism of media coverage. "The media should be embarrassed and humiliated and keep its mouth shut and just listen for a while," Bannon told a reporter. "The elite media got it dead wrong [about the 2016 election], 100% dead wrong," he added, saying this was "a humiliating defeat that they will never wash away, that will always be there." Bannon clearly enjoyed attacking the press. The tension among Trump, his people, and the media, then as now, has been palpable, sometimes even painful.

For example, when the annual black tie dinner of the White House Correspondents' Association took place in the springtime of Trump's first year in office, a few thousand card-carrying members of the Washington elite were at a big downtown Washington hotel, expecting fun-and-games between the president and the press. So it had been for thirty-six years in a row, whether the president was a Republican or a Democrat. But that year Trump turned down the association's invitation, and many of his staff, sniffing the president's hostility toward the press, decided they would also keep their distance. Instead Trump journeyed to Harrisburg, Pennsylvania, a city he'd described during the campaign as "just rotting . . . it's just a war zone," but now called a "wonderful, beautiful place." At a dinner there with local Republicans, he blasted the Washington dinner he'd chosen to stiff as a "large group of Hollywood celebrities" and the "Washington media," phrases that drew instant jeers, boos, and laughter. "I could not possibly be more thrilled than to be more than a hundred miles away from the Washington swamp," he paused, and "with much, much better people." His carefully selected audience cheered his every word of derision.

Meanwhile, in the Washington swamp, the dinner proceeded happily. The correspondents' president, Jeff Mason, told the assembled reporters: "We are not fake news. We are not failing news organizations. And we are not the enemy of the American people." The last line received a standing ovation.

Then, to the surprise of many "ink-stained wretches," as reporters were once called, Trump decided in year two of his administration that he would attend the 2018 Gridiron Dinner, where several hundred of Washington's most prominent journalists by tradition roasted the president and other senior officials, and where the president roasted the journalists—all in good fun, of course. The question was whether Trump could joke about himself, and it turned out that he could—once or twice, anyway.

Every reporter knew that Trump needed an enemy, someone to blame when things went sour. He would never accept any blame himself. He saw himself as perfect. The media was his ideal enemy. So it had been for nearly every Republican leader since Nixon's time.

Though Trump has been at war with the media, most reporters do not see themselves as being at war with the president. Most would like simply to cover him, rigorously but fairly. As *Washington Post* editor Martin Baron put it, "We're not at war; we're at work." There were others, no doubt, who would throw themselves into the task of toppling him from power.

Another contrived enemy for Trump is the "deep state," the concept first brought to the president's attention by Bannon. It was not heavy lifting for someone like Trump to believe in this fantasy—he can imagine and tweet, for example, that the Robert Mueller investigation is "the single greatest WITCH HUNT in American political history, led by some very bad and conflicted people." To find these people, he urged his cabinet officers to dig down into their departments for people who were not doing their jobs, meaning in this context people who were not loyal to administration policy and the president.

In April 2018, Trump set his sights on the State Department, a place he regarded with the deepest suspicion. As a step toward "draining the swamp," a much more difficult task than he had first imagined, he approved the hiring of Mari Stull, a beverage-lobbyist-turned-wine-blogger, who operated under the name of "Vino Vixen." She was to be a "senior adviser" to the Bureau of International Organization Affairs, based in Foggy Bottom. She quickly plunged into a quiet but determined effort to vet dozens of career diplomats as a way of checking on their loyalty to the president's agenda and policies. According to *Foreign Policy* magazine, one source disclosed, "She is gunning for American citizens in the UN to see if they are toeing the line." And if they were not, they would either be transferred to other less glamorous posts or be asked to resign.[8]

TWO

From Nero to Trump

WHEN DONALD TRUMP FIRST started using the phrase "enemy of the people," he likely had no idea that it had been a favorite of twentieth-century dictators, such as Stalin and Hitler. If he had known, would it have made any difference? Would it have persuaded him not to use it at all? My guess is that the phrase caught his fancy, and once so hooked, it satisfied his need of the moment, and he felt perfectly comfortable using it.

Still, a brief lesson for the president: The phrase did not originate with Pat Caddell; it actually goes back to the chaotic rule of Emperor Nero, who, as the saying goes, fiddled while Rome burned. He vacationed in Greece while his empire's economy collapsed and a revolt in Gaul succeeded. By the time he returned, the Roman Senate had condemned him as *hostis publicus*, public enemy, and he committed suicide. Nero, for historians, was the first recorded "enemy" of the "public," or of the people.

During the years of the French Revolution, the meaning of the phrase changed dramatically. No longer did it apply to a ruler who had gone mad with power; now it was the ruler who applied it to anyone who challenged his power. In 1794, as violence spread, a "revolutionary tribunal" was established "to punish enemies of the people" and to determine which political crimes deserved the death penalty. None was cited more than "spreading false news to divide or trouble the people." Critics of the revolution, mostly writers and intellectuals, were among those most often directed to the bloody guillotine.

The concept of "enemy of the people" moved from the guillotine to the stage in an 1882 play of that name by Norwegian writer Henrik Ibsen, reflecting a broader European confusion about its true meaning. Who was the "enemy"? The writer who criticized his government? Or the government that could not tolerate, and would not allow, any criticism? In the play, the "enemy" turned out to be an honorable, idealistic doctor who discovered contamination in the spa town's water supply and pleaded with the mayor and the press to go public with the news. They refused, fearing that the revelation would destroy the town's reputation and lead to economic disaster and popular backlash. The doctor unjustly was portrayed as an "enemy of the people."

It took the Russian Revolution in 1917 to end all doubts about who was the "enemy." The Bolsheviks, led by the fiery, abusive, totally dedicated Vladimir Lenin, seized power in November 1917 and quickly imposed censorship over all means of communication. Lenin was determined, from day one, to control the message. Then, glancing back at the model of the French Revolution, he ruled that the Jacobin terror against *vrag naroda,* Russian for "enemy of the people," was "instructive": it ought to be revived to rid "the new Russia" of "landowners and capitalists as a class." Whether they were called "landowners" or "capitalists," they were to be treated as "enemies of the people." How were "enemies" to be treated? By exile to Siberia or death.

Josef Stalin, the cold-blooded Bolshevik bureaucrat who succeeded Lenin in 1924, vastly expanded the meaning of "enemy of the people" to include anyone he considered a political rival. At the beginning, there were quite a few, among them Leon Trotsky, but then the number dwindled as Stalin killed his critics. By the mid-1930s, the phrase became the equivalent of a death sentence; so designated, millions of innocent people were banished and perished. Stalin ruled like a god, a remote and powerful leader whose image evoked fear and whose word was unquestioned. Through the rigidly controlled press, dominated by Stalin and unburdened by truth, Russia became a crazed, closed world, where talk of conspiracies replaced normal conversation and weird fantasies erupted from a Kremlin gone mad.

From Stalin's Moscow, the concept of "enemy of the people" spread to other dictatorships around the world but did not reach democracies—until now. In the 1930s, there was no more passionate an adherent than Adolf Hitler, like Stalin an absolute dictator. Historians note that, before the Nazis took power in Germany, Hitler had read, and reread, Ibsen's *Enemy of the People*, admiring it so much he actually wove a few key lines from the play into his speeches. For a determined anti-Semite like Hitler, it was only a small step to damning all Jews as "enemies of the people." His propaganda minister, Joseph Goebbels, wrote in 1941, "Each Jew is a sworn enemy of the German people." Elaborating, he added: "If someone wears the Jewish star, he is an enemy of the people. Anyone who deals with him is the same as a Jew and must be treated accordingly." The Nazis murdered 6 million Jews during World War II.

Another dictator who embraced the phrase was Mao Zedong, who imposed communism on China in 1949. He, like Lenin, was a dedicated revolutionary, and in pursuit of his Marxist dream he could be cruel. Millions died when an avoidable famine hit the countryside in the late 1950s. He blamed his critics and spent years purging them from power.

According to Zhengyuan Fu, a Chinese scholar, Chinese society was divided into two groups: the "people" and the "class enemy." The "people," according to communist lexicon, were workers, peasants, and soldiers. The "class enemies of the people" were generally writers, intellectuals, or party critics of the state's policy. The party, by theoretically associating itself with the "people," thus acquired a form of legitimacy when it crushed its "enemies."

It was always the same message: In the land of the dictator, whether in Russia or China, the critic, the reporter, was considered the "enemy of the people."

Khrushchev, Stalin, and Me

A few years after Stalin's death in March 1953, I traveled to Moscow, where I was soon to run into the phrase "enemy of the people" not as a casual encounter on Red Square but as a policy shift of monumental importance in modern Russian history. The American embassy in the Soviet capital had been in urgent need of a translator with top-secret clearance, fluent in Russian, and single. I happily fit the bill, having just completed a classified research program in Army intelligence on North Korea's brutal treatment of U.S. prisoners of war. I had been a Ph.D. student in Russian history at Harvard.

For a foreigner, Moscow has always been a place of wonder, "a riddle wrapped in a mystery inside an enigma," as Great Britain's wartime prime minister, Winston Churchill, once said. January 1956, the month I arrived, was unbelievably cold, temperatures dropping, literally, to 42 below zero; snow falling like iced confetti from skies darkened by thick gray clouds. At the U.S. embassy, the focus was on the Twentieth Congress of the Soviet Communist Party, scheduled to start on February 14, the first Congress since Stalin's death. The Soviet press hinted at dramatic political change on the near horizon. (My job was to read and analyze the Soviet press.) The phrase "cult of personality" appeared with exceptional frequency. But what did it mean?

If we were to get answers, we knew we would get them from party leader Nikita Khrushchev, a tough, unpredictable *apparatchik* who opened the Congress with a long speech filled with artificial bravado but little about the fate of Stalin's legacy—which is what the 1,355 voting and 81 nonvoting delegates wanted to know. They could not help but notice, as they entered the mammoth meeting hall, that the large photo of Stalin, which had stared down at them for decades, was now missing. If Stalin was to be downsized, then so might they be. Uncertainty, framed by fear, was etched on their faces.

Ten days later, on February 24, the Twentieth Congress officially ended. But late that night, as the delegates were packing to return home, they were suddenly summoned back to the Kremlin. Not all of them were surprised. A few sensed that their leader had left something unsaid.

Khrushchev spoke for four hours, from past midnight till before dawn. It was a speech not of literary merit but of political and historic importance. Looking "red-faced and excited," according to one observer, the pudgy, bald, perspiring Khrushchev stunned not only the assembled delegates but eventually the entire communist world by delivering a devastating, no-nonsense attack on the god-like Georgian who had run the Soviet Union for twenty-nine years. Khrushchev's biographer, William Taubman, called it "the bravest and most reckless thing he ever did. The Soviet regime never fully recovered, and neither did he."

Khrushchev said that Stalin was guilty of a "grave abuse of power." He reminded the delegates that Stalin's one-man rule, his "cult of personality," as he put it, had led to "mass arrests" and the "deportation" of "thousands and thousands of innocent people." There had been "executions without trial," creating "insecurity, fear and even desperation."

There had also been a dangerous corruption of language. Khrushchev denounced such phrases as "counter-revolutionary crimes" and "enemy of the people"—these were "absurd, wild and contrary to common sense." He said "innocent communists" had confessed "because of physical methods of pressure, torture, reducing them to unconsciousness, depriving them of judgment, taking away their human dignity." Stalin himself gave the order to torture the prisoners.[1]

It was difficult, if not impossible, for a foreigner to appreciate the full impact of Khrushchev's speech—once it became public—on the average Russian, trained over centuries to respect the awesome power of an almighty *vozhd*. Khrushchev was not simply denouncing another politician, he was denouncing a secular, untouchable god. On that night, none of us at the embassy had even an inkling of the unprecedented drama unfolding inside the Kremlin, only a few blocks away. It took three weeks for Ambassador Charles Bohlen, one of America's top diplomats, to learn about the speech. He was attending a reception at the French embassy, and his source was an Israeli diplomat. At roughly the same time, I was told by a Russian friend that delegates at the secret speech were seen popping nitroglycerin tablets into their mouths; several died of heart attacks. Everyone was left momentarily speechless, concerned not only about their own future but also about the nation's. Would it survive this seismic shock?

Khrushchev was clearly breaking precious political and ideological crockery, but, to reform the Soviet Union—which he considered an absolute necessity, else the system itself would fall apart—he felt he had to dismantle Stalin's legacy, to reduce this fake god to a human shell. Especially cruel to him was the phrase "enemy of the people," which he sought to expunge from Soviet law and party practice. "It eliminated the possibility of any kind of ideological fight," Khrushchev said, referring to the unlikely possibility of political disagreement in Stalin's Russia. "The formula 'enemy of the people' was specifically introduced for the purpose of physically annihilating individuals" who disagreed with Stalin, even communists thought to be in good standing.

In his memoir, published years later, Khrushchev wrote passionately about two communist officials, identified only as Rabinovich and Finkel, "exceptionally honorable and decent people." Thinking back, "I could never entertain even the thought that these two, . . . whom I knew extremely well, might really be 'enemies of the people.' But 'factual material' was concocted against all those who were arrested, and I had no possibility of refuting it. All I did then was curse myself for letting myself be fooled. Here were these men who had been closely associated with me, and now they were called 'enemies of the people.'" Khrushchev also mentioned a Korytny, a Kiev party official "tested and proved in the Civil War, but still he was arrested" and accused of being an "enemy of the people."

For many years, during the 1930s and 1940s, Khrushchev had tolerated the use of "enemy of the people" and watched as many were marched off to death camps in Siberia. But then he could not tolerate it any longer, and he broke with his own ignominious past, delivering his remarkable speech at the Twentieth Congress. His conscience could finally claim a victory.

Khrushchev remained a communist, but a troubled one, aware of the frailties and problems in Marxism/Leninism, yet determined to pursue its doomed course. Three years after his speech, in 1959, I covered as a CBS reporter the debates Khrushchev organized with the traveling U.S. vice president, Richard Nixon. In one debate, which was covered by television, a relatively new form of news in the Soviet Union, Khrushchev exploded with the wildly hyped projection that, because communism in his judgment would one day be victorious over capitalism on the world stage, Nixon's grandchildren would live in a communist state. It was the inexorable flow of history, he proclaimed. No other result was possible. Nixon, of course, took the contrary position, and he proved to be far more prescient than Khrushchev. No, he said, your grandchildren will live under capitalism.

Proof in 2018 lay in two different cities, both in the United States. Khrushchev's son, Sergei, lived comfortably in Cranston, Rhode Island, after a long and distinguished teaching career at Brown University, and Khrushchev's great granddaughter, Nina, lived in New York, an admired professor of international relations at the New School. Both often visited Russia, now a country still struggling to find a post-communist identity, but they lived in the United States.

Nixon's "Enemies List"

A courageous journalist named Endre Marton was also born in a communist country but escaped to the United States after the 1956 Hungarian rebellion against Soviet rule. For years,

Marton, working for the Associated Press, had covered events in Hungary. Like a handful of other East European countries, Hungary was a reluctant member of the Warsaw Pact, a military alliance under Moscow's control. A keen observer of politics and diplomacy, Marton produced objective accounts of Communist Party plans and projects but also stories of power struggles, corruption, and bureaucratic inefficiency that profoundly angered party leaders. Unable to tame Marton, they jailed him. The Hungarian secret police labeled him and his family "the sworn enemies of our People's Democracy and faithful adherents of the American way of life, and, though they pursue their professional work openly, their reporting is mocking and hostile to our national interest." Their story appeared in *Enemies of the People*, a book by Marton's talented journalist daughter, Kati.

Here was another example of an autocratic regime, unwilling to accept criticism, condemning a reporter to prison for doing his job.

When the brave, experienced Marton reached the United States, the AP made a quick decision. Marton was assigned, appropriately, to the State Department, where he covered American foreign policy for many years. It was where I met him and where we shared many stories about the dos and don'ts of reporting on regimes that have little or no respect for the concept of freedom, especially when applied to the press.

We both covered the Nixon administration's foreign policy, which focused on exploiting tensions between Russia and China to help end the Vietnam War on terms satisfying to Richard Nixon's sense of national honor. Though Nixon realized, even before taking office, that military victory in Vietnam was unattainable, he continued the fight (more than 28,000 Americans were killed on his watch), while he bombed his way to a humiliating defeat in 1975. As CBS's chief diplomatic correspondent at the time, I was on air frequently. My reports about the war, I was told, infuriated the president, and, as a result, my phones were tapped, my income tax returns were audited five years in a row (not a cent out of line), and my CBS office at the State Department was twice ransacked. Nixon even wanted me tailed when I covered the Paris peace talks in 1968, but FBI director J. Edgar Hoover, of all people, killed the idea, claiming it would be too expensive. Six agents would have to be assigned to cover one reporter. It made no sense, thought Hoover.

Nixon also put me on his "enemies list," which, considering the high quality of the others so placed, I always considered a distinct honor. I guess Nixon's "enemies list" was his way of labeling journalists—those who pointed out the fallacies and fantasies in his policies—as "enemies of the people." He should have known better. He was an experienced politician, but one plagued by deep insecurities that led him to engage in illegal actions during the Watergate scandal. He loved his country, but brought shame upon it and himself by regarding criticism as dissent and dissent as disloyalty.

THREE

"The Appalling Becomes Excusable"

MANY AMERICANS WANTED TO believe that Donald Trump, once in office and facing the awesome responsibilities of the presidency, would finally become a president around whom the nation could rally. Maybe, they hoped, he would stop tweeting about matters of war and peace. He would quit ad-libbing policy as if he were on a talk show. He would do his homework. He would read his briefing books. He would turn off cable television. He would prepare for meetings with foreign leaders. He would live up to his self-proclaimed reputation as a "great negotiator" and deal sensibly with Congress. He would, at the end of the day, understand that there is a vast difference between campaigning, when winning an election defines success, and governing, when balancing sharply competing interests at home and abroad defines success.

But Trump, at age seventy-two, has not changed, and the nation has not rallied around him. His poll numbers are among the lowest any president has had at this time in office since World War II. Nothing that he says or does comes as a complete shock any longer. Yet he is still capable of surprising everyone, whether in Washington or Beijing or anyplace else, which makes him interesting, unsettling, and even frightening. He is president of the United States, arguably the most powerful politician in the world. His words and actions matter.

When, shortly after placing his hand on the Bible and swearing his allegiance to the U.S. Constitution, he began to attack the press as an "enemy of the American people," he had to be taken seriously. A larger question had to be addressed, too: If he did not know or appreciate the importance of a free press in guaranteeing the foundation of American democracy, might he not also arrogantly challenge the independence of the judiciary, belittle judges, demean and fire a director of the Federal Bureau of Investigation, even criticize as "Nazis" those intelligence agents who kept the nation's secrets? And this was exactly what he did—all in the interest of protecting his presidency and himself from the results of officially authorized investigations into his volatile 2016 presidential campaign.

Offering a variety of excuses and explanations, some of which made no sense, Trump has undercut fundamental institutions of American democracy, severely damaging the FBI, the Department of Justice, and even key committees of Congress—all of which were once noted for their independence from the White House. He has also, like an uppercut to the jaw, rattled American leadership in the world. Where once, pre-Trump, most nations looked to Washington for guidance, now they look elsewhere, sharply reducing American influence in key parts of the world. The White House, once seen as a majestic house of democracy and freedom, has now, under

Trump, come to symbolize corruption and self-centered in-effectiveness. Indeed, more than anything else, the ominous cloud of possible collusion between Trump and the Russians has hung over him and the country from his first day in office, and, until it is resolved, one way or another, will probably do so to his last day.

If possible, what worries many Americans even more is that we have been getting used to Trump's unorthodox style of governance. We no longer feel disgraced; we have become accustomed to what was once unimaginable; it's now being called the new norm. "The appalling becomes excusable," explained *New York Times* columnist Roger Cohen, "the heinous becomes debatable, the outrageous becomes comical, lies become fibs, spite becomes banal, and hymns to American might become cause for giddy chants of national greatness." Because everything around us seems to look the same (the job hasn't changed, the lamp post is still on the corner, the flag still flies from the White House roof, the president still delivers a State of the Union address), we grow increasingly accustomed to Trump's alarming changes in governance and accept them as almost normal. There have been so many of them, embracing his management of American policy, that many of us just shrug and look the other way.

In domestic policy, for example, Trump has tangled repeatedly and embarrassingly with Congress, even though Republicans controlled both houses. They blundered for much of the first year, trying to repeal the Affordable Care Act, often referred to as Obamacare, and, in desperation, as Christmas hovered over their meager legislative accomplishments, they rammed a $1.5 trillion tax cut on straight party-line votes through Congress without hearings, in large measure so Trump and the GOP could lay claim to a political victory despite the bill's glaring tilt toward unfairly benefiting the super-wealthy.

And, following Bannon's guidance on "deconstructing the establishment," Trump has launched a massive effort to eviscerate a wide range of government agencies, especially in the scientific and environmental fields, with the stated purpose of returning government "to the people," but actually weakening public protections and resulting in less research at universities and more harm to public health. "Consumer Watchdog Unit Stripped of Power" was a *Washington Post* headline on February 2, 2018, typical of Trump's devastating assault on all agencies responsible for protecting the health and well-being of Americans, notably the underprivileged.

In foreign policy, with his "America First" pledge uppermost on his mind, Trump immediately pulled the United States out of the Trans-Pacific Partnership (TPP), fulfilling a promise he had made during the campaign. He argued that this huge free trade agreement, negotiated by presidents George W. Bush and Barack Obama, was a "job killer." Actually, by withdrawing, the United States opened the door to China to play an even larger role in Asia's expanding economy. "Without America: Australia in the New Asia" was the title of Australian analyst Hugh White's widely read judgment of Asia in the Trump era. But in April 2018, Trump appeared to flip on the TPP, announcing that he might change his mind on his original decision and try now to negotiate a new agreement more favorable to the United States.

Stunning America's allies even more was Trump's announcement that he was going to impose a 25 percent tariff on imported steel and a 10 percent tariff on imported aluminum. In a rare display of courage, Speaker of the House Paul Ryan rose to object to the president's plan, warning it could trigger a dangerous trade war. The president proceeded anyway, but only after temporarily exempting key allies and trading partners.

Of even greater long-term consequence, Trump also withdrew from the nonbinding Paris climate accords. This unilateral step raised questions about America's role in containing the catastrophic effects of global warming and made it easier for China to claim the mantle of global leadership.

Trump played games with the crucially important Article 5 of the NATO treaty, which obliges all member states to come to the aid of any member state asking for their assistance. The article has been invoked just once: on behalf of the United States, after the September 2011 terrorist attacks. Despite that history, at a NATO meeting in the spring of 2017 Trump deliberately refused to pledge America's commitment to Article 5, sending more shivers of uncertainty through the alliance than at any other time since its founding in 1948. Upsetting everyone, which might have been his intent, he reluctantly made the pledge but in a tone of bewildering obfuscation that left many of his allies scratching their heads. Was he for Article 5 or not? they wondered. The answer is still not clear.

North Korea presented an example of a "clear and present danger" to Trump. If there was uncertainty elsewhere on his horizon, there was none here. When Barack Obama handed the White House keys to the new president, he warned Trump that North Korea, specifically its young, unpredictable leader, Kim Jong Un, was a building crisis that would likely explode in the early days of the new administration. And, within days of his inauguration, the new president received intelligence strongly suggesting North Korea was on an accelerated schedule to build nuclear-armed missiles that could hit the United States. Trump, through tweet and thunderous proclamation, tried to frighten Kim into abandoning his nuclear program, but it became clear after a while that this approach was failing.

In the buildup to the 2018 Winter Olympics in Seoul, North and South Korea took matters into their own hands. First they agreed to combine their Olympic teams into one, and then they plunged into a secret negotiation that produced the surprising proposal for a U.S.-North Korea summit meeting, which Trump instantly accepted. After off-again, on-again gamesmanship, the two unpredictable leaders met in Singapore for a one-day summit on June 12. It was hailed by both Trump and Kim as historic, and hundreds of reporters covered the handshakes and smiles. Both Trump and Kim acted as if they had been friends all their lives, ignoring more than a year of bitter mutual insults. When reporters described what was obvious—that much of the talk was no more than artificial hype—an angry Trump ripped into the press, fingering NBC and CNN especially, for "fake" reporting. "Our country's biggest enemy," he charged, hours after meeting with one of the world's most vicious dictators, "is the Fake News so easily promulgated by fools."[1] The president who had earlier called the press "the enemy of the American people" now upped the intensity of his attack to describe it as the "country's biggest enemy," leaving many with the impression that Trump was not really a serious person.

For those who thought the two countries were heading toward war, this was a head-turning change, but one still loaded with uncertainties. Now, suddenly, diplomacy was being given a chance to settle a very difficult problem. Would Trump be able to demonstrate the skill, knowledge, and patience required to do the job? And would Kim be able to retain his nuclear shield, even after the summit, and also attract Western assistance, so desperately needed for his failing economy?

Trump always claimed that he knew more about diplomatic strategy than anyone else, and he banked on his personal ability to win Xi Jinping of China and Vladimir Putin of Russia to support his approach toward North Korea and other global problems. Trump met with both Xi and Putin. Once he traveled to China, where he was accorded royal treatment, which he relished. He also joined Putin in a controversial one-on-one summit in Helsinki, Finland, in July 2018. Many pundits and politicians criticized Trump for bowing to Putin's personality and policies. Both Xi and Putin used flattery as a tool of diplomacy, playing to Trump's ego, and he took the flattery to be proof of his diplomatic skills. But he was kidding himself, and he might have been the only one who didn't know it.

"The Greatest President since Washington"

The president's track record in foreign and domestic policy has been problematic at best. It has created unnecessary and serious problems for the country and diminished its stature around the world. Of course, Trump has a completely different opinion of his presidency. He thinks it is the "greatest" of all time. He enjoys quoting Orrin Hatch of Utah, the longest-serving GOP senator.

"He said once, I'm the greatest living president in his lifetime," the president boasted. "He actually once said, 'I'm the greatest president in the history of the country.'

"And I said, 'Does that include Lincoln and Washington?'

"He said, 'Yes.'

"I said, 'I love this guy.'"

Hatch's office issued a quick correction, saying Hatch meant Trump "may" become the "greatest" the American history. But Trump's sense of self is so limitless, like horizons without end, that he allows himself to believe such claptrap and to spread it as gospel. This White House lives on Kellyanne Conway's "alternative facts," and sometimes no facts at all. One aide, Scottie Nell Hughes, said, "There is no such thing, unfortunately, anymore as facts," contradicting the long-established wisdom of the late New York senator Daniel Patrick Moynihan, who said you can have your own opinions, but not your own facts. "Alternative facts," post-fact, fake news, fake polls—this is all very dangerous. Trump's chaotic rule should not be allowed to become the accepted norm of government performance.

In my judgment, there is a crying need for change, and the sooner the better, but only through proper constitutional means. There is no reason to hope that Trump, in disgust, tired of the workload, and increasingly depressed by legal challenges and blistering criticism, will resign prior to the end of his first term in office.

On the contrary, Trump has been encouraged to believe that he is God's gift to America by a blaring symphony of support from a conservative media empire now more powerful than ever, ready to echo the president's latest pronouncements, whatever they may be. GOP senator Joseph McCarthy of Wisconsin, another rabble-rousing demagogue who attracted extensive coverage while leading an anticommunist witch-hunt in the early 1950s, could have benefited from such media support, but he could not have it—it did not yet exist!

Since, for Trump, this media empire is an elixir for the ego, a source of knowledge and ideas, he doesn't need thick folders from the CIA to tell him what is happening in Yemen or Syria or the South China Sea, or what Putin's strategic plans might be, or what the Taliban are now planning for Afghanistan. He can ride with his gut feelings, his instant likes and dislikes, and know he will have widespread support from the 40 percent of the American electorate who have been in his hip pocket since the day of his election.

In the week of the U.S.-North Korea summit announcement and the steel and aluminum tariff threat, Trump was operating on his own, doing, according to Jonathan Swan of *Axios*, "what he wants, when he wants, how he wants." A *Washington Post* headline writer put it this way: "President Acts as Own Diplomat, Negotiator," and the Associated Press said, "In the tough times, Trump goes it alone." Swan paraphrased a "senior administration official," who admired Trump, as saying, "No single individual in history has been able to direct an entire news cycle on a whim, and he's using that power at his sole discretion, with the WH policy press, and comms teams just along for the ride." It might have been an amazing one-man spectacle for the official, but for Trump, who always considered himself "the man on the white horse," this was just a day at the office.

Sean Hannity and Laura Ingraham on Fox News, Rush Limbaugh on radio, *Breitbart* for exclusive reports on conspiracies hatched by illegal Muslim terrorists, the *Drudge Report* for breaking gossip, and many more posing as news and commentary outlets—at any moment, they can produce a loud chorus of support for anything Trump proposes or claims.

If, for example, Trump suddenly believes that the FBI, once considered untouchable by conservatives, has now become a "deep state" nest of liberals and Democrats, and the nest must be eradicated, almost all of his right-wing media chorus would instantly be ready to follow his lead, no questions asked.

The Trump chorus is heard and seen on many outlets, none

more influential, though, than the Fox cable news network. The "alternative" universe of MSNBC is reserved mostly for liberals. Hannity seems to speak for Fox, Rachel Maddow for MSNBC. On any given evening, a major issue is joined, and another rhetorical battle fought. What makes this split-screen warfare so meaningful is that everyone knows Trump is watching, and important policy decisions often get made in this magical moment of virtually nonstop TV viewing.

The McCarthy Parallel

On April 10, 2018, the CNN website warned of "dark and unprecedented times ahead." The reason was that the night before the FBI had taken the highly unusual step of raiding the offices, home, and hotel room of Michael Cohen, the president's personal lawyer and ultimate supporter. The raids suggested that the Department of Justice had compelling evidence of bank fraud or campaign finance illegalities that might link President Trump to Cohen's decision weeks before the 2016 election to buy the silence of a porn star and a *Playboy* model. Both women claimed extramarital affairs with the president years before his election. Within days, the Justice Department added to the drama by disclosing that Cohen was, in fact, "under criminal investigation."

Once again, Washington went into overdrive. Was this the moment when Trump would fire Special Counsel Robert Mueller? Or Attorney General Jeff Sessions? Or Sessions's deputy, Rod Rosenstein, who had approved of the FBI raid? Certainly he was thinking about it. And, if he did, would the constitutional crisis, the updated Saturday Night Massacre so widely forecast, actually be at hand? Or might this all be just another false alarm, bells and whistles about one subject suddenly displaced by the excitement of another hot tweet hours later? None of this has yet been etched into history, but what seems clear is that Trump, one way or the other, might some day face his personal and political Armageddon. His immediate reaction to the FBI raid was an emotional eruption so volcanic in power that only his family and close White House aides had ever seen or heard anything like it before. He was described as "furious," "angry," for the moment "uncontrolled." Up to this point, Trump had had to worry only about congressional investigations, which he thought he could contain, and Mueller's, which was always an advancing question mark. Now a new one, centered on his New York consigliere, was added, and it might prove to be the most devastating of them all.

Making matters worse, Trump had been absorbed with a set of delicate and dangerous deliberations about what action, military and/or diplomatic, he would take against Bashar al-Assad's regime in Syria following reports that once again the Syrian strongman had used a form of poison gas against his rebel opponents, in the process killing dozens of women and children. To convey the image of a president deeply involved in affairs of state, not of the heart, the White House press office had invited TV cameras into the Cabinet Room to record the scene. But instead of focusing on the Syria crisis, Trump, unable to control his temper, lashed out at the FBI and warned he might be close to firing Special Counsel Mueller, thus opening the door to a possible constitutional crisis. "It's a disgrace," Trump roared, "frankly, a real disgrace." He paused for only a moment. "Why don't I just fire Mueller?" he asked rhetorically. "Well, I think it's a disgrace what is going on. We'll see what happens. . . . Many people have said, you should fire him." He left the question hanging, like a bomb about to explode.

The following morning, Trump continued his tweet response to the FBI raid. "Attorney-client privilege is dead!" he pronounced prematurely. Then he switched back to the Mueller investigation. In capital letters, he wrote, "A TOTAL WITCH HUNT!!!" No one could miss the import of the capital letters and three exclamation points.

Trump's threats filled the front pages of the major newspapers. Pundits, pro- and anti-Trump, echoed these threats on cable news shows. Ratings on Fox and MSNBC soared as tempers flared, and conservative critics made the case that, indeed, the FBI needed a spring cleaning. Maybe the Justice Department and the State Department also needed a cleaning. All of this conjured up visions of a McCarthy-type assault on the legal underpinnings of American democracy. Back of it all, it seemed, was another effort by the president to derail the Mueller investigation and save both himself and his presidency.

Would Trump succeed? The accumulated evidence suggests the answer could be yes. Trump might very well succeed in saving himself—at least temporarily—by undermining the legitimacy of the FBI, the Justice Department, and even Congress, led, paradoxically, by his own party. Republican politicians seemed more intent on protecting their embattled president and winning the next election than on figuring out a proper American response to proven Russian interference in the 2016 presidential election. As for possible "collusion" between the Trump campaign and the Russian government, it was considered so controversial that GOP politicians fled from any serious discussion of the subject and Trump simply dismissed it as a "hoax."

Trump, rather than defend the FBI, has undermined its credibility and legitimacy. Answering questions about the FBI's role, Trump, head down, scowled, "I think it's terrible.

It's a disgrace what's happening in our country. A lot of people should be ashamed of themselves. And much worse than that." He repeatedly hinted that top officials at the Justice Department might be fired. As always, he protected no one but himself, and not very effectively.

Senator John McCain, chair of the Senate Armed Services Committee, battling cancer and spending more time at home in Arizona, was one of the few Republicans willing to take on Trump and the timid party leaders. In February 2018 he tweeted, "The latest attacks on the FBI and Department of Justice serve no American interests—no party's, no president's, only Putin's." McCain kept his finger on a key pulsating issue: Russian interference in the 2016 presidential campaign, despite Trump's efforts to belittle its importance.

In April 2018, Trump flew to White Sulphur Springs, West Virginia, to deliver a speech on taxes, the lowering of which has been holy writ for Republicans since Ronald Reagan. Briefly, at a roundtable gathering, he touched on taxes, praised himself, and then, in a bit of staged theatricality, threw his prepared comments into the air, pages scattering to the floor, and muttered, with feigned tiredness, "This would have been a little boring." He wanted to be the star of something exciting, ready-made for the evening TV news programs. So, suddenly, like the TV host he once was, he switched topics—from taxes to old-fashioned politics. He attacked the state's popular Democratic senator, Joe Manchin, and warned illegal immigrants that he was going to "throw" them all into "the paddy wagon." He regurgitated what he considered classics from his 2016 presidential campaign, including the size of his inauguration crowd and the wall he was going to build along the Mexican border—classics that, clearly, he thought, deserved to be memorialized in capital letters in a book he would one day write, perhaps called "Trump—How I Cleaned the Swamp, When No One Else Could!"

A presidential performance? Hardly, but Trumpian to its core. In the annals of American history, Donald Trump may be described as an original. As *The Economist* noted, the organizing principle of his presidency is loyalty—not to a vision or a principle but to himself. All presidents are vain, to one degree or another, the magazine acknowledged, but Trump has raised vanity to Olympian heights while dragging the fundamental institutions of American democracy—the sanctity of the law and the vitality of a free press—into a wobbly state of defensive uncertainty. Both institutions continue to do their jobs responsibly, on occasion even brilliantly, but they remain under fire from a president who likewise is under fire, creating a political environment noted as much for subpoenas, a special counsel, congressional investigations, and a chaotic White House than for legislation, humanitarian pride, and national security.

The question then has often been asked: "Has there ever been another president like Trump?" The answer might well be, "Fortunately, no!" But the question keeps being asked, and must be addressed.

Since Trump was inaugurated as president in January 2017, hardly a day goes by when I have not heard, or joined, a discussion of Trump this or Trump that. He seems to be everywhere, which clearly is where he wants to be. But even if there has not been an equivalent predecessor to Trump, has there not been a close parallel, someone or some moment when the nation's politics were thrown into chaotic disarray by a president or by a politician who aspired to be president?

Of course, in all of these discussions, Richard Nixon's name bubbles predictably to the top of the list, and it is sure to kick off a lively debate about glaring failures mixed uncomfortably with undoubted successes. In any comparison with Trump, there are many parallels—Nixon's penchant for lying, his frequent flirtation with illegal acts, his war on the press, his slippery challenges to the U. S. Constitution. But there are differences, too, and they are meaningful. Nixon was an experienced politician, a pro who respected the system, even as he tried to subvert it. He had served in the military. He had been elected to office not once but many times. He had served as a congressman, a senator, a vice president, and finally as president. He had been through the hoops. Trump, by contrast, was in his own, very different world—a real estate huckster for whom public service was as foreign as an immigrant from a "shithole" country in Africa.

A step or two behind Nixon lies the broader Watergate scandal that consumed his administration and ultimately led to his resignation in August 1974, under the shadow of almost certain impeachment. Here, Watergate parallels Trumpgate, but history, when finally written, may well put the Nixon scandal in second place. Trumpgate appears to be galloping far ahead of the politics of Watergate, keeping the nation (and the world) enthralled in legal battles, diplomatic machinations, and low-life business deals and sex scandals. If Watergate attracted hundreds of book contracts (and still counting), Trumpgate may well attract thousands. It is that much more complicated and, for a writer or journalist, that much more compelling a subject.

And, interestingly, in this lineup of possible parallels, one also hears, with increasing frequency, the name of Senator Joseph McCarthy of Wisconsin, the scowling author in the early 1950s of an unorthodox anticommunist crusade that for several years frightened the nation and, for a time, handcuffed even President Dwight Eisenhower into embarrassing inaction. McCarthy's irresponsible bluster, his nonstop lying, his ego-driven speechifying, his campaign against the press—all of this seemingly intended to put the senator, in his own mind anyway, perilously close to a run for the Oval Office. In 1954, before his collapse, McCarthy was the second most popular Republican in the country. Eisenhower, the general who became president, was, of course, the first. In retrospect, McCarthy's actions also seemed eerily to foreshadow Trump's platform of creeping authoritarianism.

When Peter Beinart, journalist and professor at the City University of New York, published an article in *The Atlantic* titled "The New McCarthyism of Donald Trump" in July 2015, just as Trump was descending his faux gold escalator in the Trump Tower to enter the 2016 campaign, he was reasonably certain that no Republican candidate could become the GOP presidential nominee—and win the presidency—after criticizing the esteemed Senator John McCain for being captured during the Vietnam War. "Impossible!" many pundits proclaimed with remarkable self-confidence. Since Trump seemed to Beinart to be so much like McCarthy—so "opportunistic," so much the "zealot," the "demagogue," always on a search for scapegoats, ready at the drop of a hat for alignment with bigots, charging, with no evidence whatever, that Barack Obama was not really an American—he could not win. Trump was, in Beinart's vision, dry, cold toast. McCarthy had lost in 1954, Trump would in 2016! Why? Because, Beinart replied, he "jumped the shark." The country was not yet ready for a Trump. But one day, he predicted, with commendable caution, "someone in the Trump/McCarthy mold" would "come along." One did in 2016, leaving many Americans wondering what was happening to their country's politics.[2]

Even after Trump knocked off one Republican candidate after another, from seventeen aspirants down to one, many pundits, both liberals and conservatives, were left puzzled. What was going on? Even after Trump won the Republican nomination for president in July 2016, they were still puzzled. Something was going on, but what? And even after Trump won the presidential election on November 8, stunning everyone, probably deep down including Trump, pundits had obvious trouble for months explaining Trump's triumph and then adjusting to the new political realities suddenly tumbling down on the nation. In fact, so close and so unexpected was the final result that many Americans, certainly those who voted for Hillary Clinton, had difficulty well into 2017 attaching the word "President" to the name "Trump." For them, the two words, "President Trump," taken together, were the equivalent of a fatal disease. The partisan split, which had divided American politics for decades, only widened further as Trump and his troops stormed into Washington, taking the nation and the world hostage to his chaotic, authoritarian style of leadership.

As had been the case during the presidential campaign, Trump had almost total control of the news cycle during the first year of this unorthodox presidency. He was the center of the news. Nothing seemed able to elbow him out of the limelight. Only in the second year, 2018, were historians and columnists able to capture a moment or two from Trump's domination of the Washington swamp to come up with a historical parallel to today's political upheaval. They fingered the Nixon experience, of course, and they pointed to Watergate. But many of them, not in intellectual exhaustion but after due deliberation, also started to study the period in the early 1950s of post–World War II America for a possible parallel—and found one in the

McCarthyism that propelled a freshman senator from Wisconsin into the forefront of American politics and spawned a Red Scare that literally terrified the nation. CNN's outspoken Jake Tapper, who seemed always absorbed with Trump's antics, wrote a best-selling thriller set in the parallel universe of Joe McCarthy's Washington.

Jon Meacham's remarkable *The Soul of America* reached deeper into American history for other troubling examples of national unease only to discover that each time, the United States recovered its balance and emerged a better country, its soul restored to its earlier greatness. That does not necessarily mean that after Trump's departure from the scene, whenever that be, all will again be well. History moves in irregular and unpredictable patterns. Trump may leave a governmental structure so radically transformed that America's soul will have lost its former magic. But at the moment we don't know.

James and Tom Risen, writing for the *New York Times* in June 2017, were among the first journalists to see and appreciate comparisons between Trump and McCarthy. In a piece titled "Donald Trump Does His Best Joe McCarthy Impression," they noted that the Republican candidate flew to Wheeling, West Virginia, where McCarthy had launched his anticommunist movement, and nearby delivered a dark speech about the Islamic State ("spreading like wildfire"), torture ("I don't think it's tough enough"), and "threats" to the nation, such as NAFTA, Mexican immigrants, and China. America faced many threats, and only he, Trump stressed, could possibly save the nation. Trump deliberately walked in McCarthy's footsteps, practicing an updated version of the senator's politics of fear. His political base, in particular white voters without college degrees, was frightened by the "others"—Muslims and Hispanics for Trump, communists for McCarthy.[3]

A West Virginia University professor, Scott Crichlow, was quoted as saying that the noncollege-educated white voter represented a larger percentage of the state's population than in any other state. "Clearly there is an audience for speeches," he told the Risens, "that rally nationalist causes and against amorphous perceived threats. What I think may be driving some of the appeal of the politics of fear is the state's low education and demographics."

Trump supporters, like Trump's campaign slogan, wanted to "make America great again" by returning America to what the Risens called "the halcyon days of the 1950s," the decade of the fearmongering Joe McCarthy.

Several months later, on October 24, Arizona's other Republican senator, Jeff Flake, delivered a speech in Congress that a romantic part of him clearly hoped would be picked up by the pundits and hailed as another "Declaration of Conscience," similar to the one that Margaret Chase Smith, the Senate's only woman at the time, delivered on June 1, 1950, to take on McCarthy's politics of "hate and character assassination." Dramatically denouncing Trump's "politics of fear," Flake insisted that he was motivated by "conscience and principle," and "as such, loyalty to conscience and principle should supersede loyalty to any man or party" (read: Trump and the GOP).

Although Flake spoke eloquently and passionately against the sitting president of his own party, he nevertheless continued to vote the party line, supporting Trump's battle against Obamacare, his selection of a Supreme Court justice, and his budget-busting tax cuts. Words have their special power, but votes on major pieces of legislation have even more power. Flake approached a plateau of courage but ultimately failed to stand on it.

Still, by recalling the courage of Senator Margaret Chase

Smith to speak out against McCarthy's "four horsemen of calumny—fear, ignorance, bigotry and smear," Flake wanted to be seen as a brave and bold senator aligned with a voice of conscience from the not-too-distant GOP past.

Flake's protest had only a temporary impact, just as Senator Smith's brave speech had failed to halt the roar of McCarthyism across the political landscape, inflicting, according to Princeton history professor Kevin M. Kruse, "incalculable damage to American political culture and political institutions." Except for a handful of prominent journalists, led by CBS's Edward R. Murrow, few in Washington or anywhere else displayed the courage of a Smith from Maine to stand up to a McCarthy from Wisconsin. If Flake was to learn anything from the Smith example, it was that personal courage, when limited to delivering one good speech, might have only minimal effect on a president or a rampaging fellow senator. Flake could have looked toward his Arizona colleague for an example of courage that leapfrogged the power of a speech. John McCain's vote to frustrate Trump's legislative plans for destroying Obamacare—that took political courage and guts!

When *Washington Post* columnist Richard Cohen scanned the political horizon in early 2018, he concluded that once again, as it had during the McCarthy era, the Republican Party had gone off the rails. In the old days, the GOP gladly supported the FBI and its untouchable director, J. Edgar Hoover. After all, Hoover happily supplied classified information to McCarthy and his notorious counsel, Roy Cohn. Now Trump attacks the FBI, accusing it, in effect, of being in league with a Democratic "deep state." He, and his conservative loyalists, seem to be reeling from jarring financial and cultural changes, such as the widespread acceptance of same-sex marriage and tussles over who gets to use what bathroom. In their view, immigrants have become, in Cohen's words, "the functional equivalent of communists. . . . The present feels unfamiliar, and the future appears frightening."

Cohen finds remarkable similarities between Trump's America and McCarthy's. He also finds today's GOP startlingly similar to McCarthy's, with the few remaining moderates, so called, cautious about standing up to the extremists. Like Mitch McConnell in the Senate and Paul Ryan in the House, establishment Republicans have decided to bow humbly before the emperor Trump, who, it is now obvious, controls the Republican Party. "History can indeed repeat itself," Cohen concludes.[4]

"Will the Trump presidency turn out to be Watergate, McCarthyism or something else entirely?" asks a Brookings essay by scholar Elaine Kamarck, who worked in the Clinton White House. Of all the possibilities, Kamarck seems to lean toward McCarthyism as the political movement that most closely resembles Trump's, though she remains cautious about final judgments. The Wisconsin senator "lied, he denied people due process, and he thwarted the rules and norms of the Senate," just as Trump has been doing. He "seems to be channeling McCarthy," which she considers hardly surprising, since both McCarthy and Trump depended on counsel Roy Cohn. Trump has what Kamarck calls a "loose relationship with facts." He lies, in other words, much as McCarthy did.[5]

Other scholars and observers have also been comparing Trump with McCarthy. It has become a fairly standard comparison, and no one making it sees it in a positive light. Carl Bernstein, who, with Bob Woodward, covered the Watergate scandal for the *Washington Post*, stated, "We may well have not seen such dark days for American democracy and its institutions since the days of Joe McCarthy." It becomes more important with each day of news bulletins, legal finagling, and congressional hearings to learn more about the McCarthy era. Through that experience, we may all learn more about the Trump era. Something similar to what happened in one era may now be happening in another.

In both eras, the American press played a major role in describing and analyzing the politics and personalities who composed the top echelons of the Republican Party. From their coverage, the American people have benefited greatly. Between then and now, though, the press has undergone a revolutionary change. Television was just getting started during the McCarthy era. CBS's Edward R. Murrow was the most influential reporter of his day. His reporting on McCarthy had a profound effect on the senator's career and legacy. Today, television is considered old hat—social media are the "in" technology—and yet, in one form or another, television remains central to the public's appreciation of Trump's actions and decisions.

In this light, McCarthy's career deserves a fresh look, as do Murrow's epic confrontations with McCarthy. If there had been no Murrow, focusing television cameras on McCarthy, the Wisconsin senator might well have continued to do even greater damage to American democracy. But Murrow took on the McCarthy challenge, and, with a series of devastating TV and radio programs and commentaries, exposed McCarthy as a cowardly and dangerous fraud. Within a few months, the senator was censured by Congress, and his notorious career was brought to a shattering end.

Murrow's role in this exciting story pulsates with professionalism and courage. He did what the best of journalism could do in the McCarthy era. Would it be realistic to hope that the best of journalism today could do a similar job of exposing President Trump as a dangerous fraud? Or, given the profound changes in communication technologies in the age of the internet, is it any longer possible that a Murrow, or a Woodward and Bernstein, could emerge, command a major national audience, and be accepted as authentic, authoritative arbiters of the truth?

FOUR

The Comparison Is Unmistakable

IT WAS EARLY FEBRUARY 1950, and Joseph McCarthy was in a hurry. The junior senator from Wisconsin, a big, beefy man with a cackle for a laugh, had fought with the Marines during World War II, been elected to the United States Senate in November 1946, and still, in his mind, had accomplished little. No legislation carried his name, and no reporters came knocking at his door. This would not do. McCarthy was wildly ambitious, a midwestern Republican, totally unprincipled, given to hyped exaggerations and outright fabrications. He was on the hunt for a hot cause, one that would produce instant gratification, controversy, and headlines for himself.

He found it, oddly, in the Cold War, which he described as the "final, all-out battle between . . . our western Christian world and the atheistic Communist world." If he could exploit it, cleverly playing on the "Red Scare" then sweeping through the land, he thought he could be propelled from the relative obscurity of the congressional backbench to the center of American politics. But how exactly, especially for someone with little intellectual curiosity and even less interest in reading? McCarthy decided that he would be utterly outrageous. With or without supporting evidence, he would name names, claiming that certain government officials were communist sympathizers or actual communists working to undermine the U.S. government.

He would accuse President Harry Truman of being "soft on communism" and Secretary of State Dean Acheson of being guilty of "the most abominable of all crimes—high treason."

In time, McCarthy would go even further, charging that the entire State Department, even the U.S. Army, was "infested" (soon to be his favorite verb) with "communist sympathizers." He would also level similar charges against university scholars, scientific researchers, and Hollywood movie producers and actors. McCarthy would crisscross the country, giving one speech after another about the communist threat to America—so many, in fact, that the name McCarthy would soon become synonymous with the struggle against "communist infiltration and subversion" of the U.S. government. He would personalize the struggle, hoping that one day the headline writers would have no alternative but to christen it *McCarthyism*—which, of course, in his mind would have a very positive ring.

Enlisting the Media to Promote the Red Scare

That was the senator's bold plan. But for it to succeed, he would have to find a way to harness the potent powers of the press, especially the new technology called television. McCarthy assumed—correctly, as it turned out—that the press, which had largely ignored him, would soon begin to cover his attacks on "communist infiltration" of the U.S. government. The more the press knew about him and covered him, the more reporters would, unwittingly, be complicit in advancing McCarthy's own anticommunist agenda. McCarthy was, after all, a U.S. senator, and the Cold War was a headline-catching story. Espionage was in the air; spies were being arrested and charged with slipping nuclear secrets to the Russians. Indeed, it could be argued that it would have been professionally irresponsible of journalists *not* to cover the junior senator from Wisconsin, since his attacks only reflected the street-corner uneasiness many Americans felt, first, about the communist threat in general (the Red Scare, as it was called), and second, about President Truman's response to it.

In a word, McCarthy, like the twenty-first-century president who also speaks and acts like a demagogue, hated the press as much as he exploited it, playing with reporters one minute as if they were enemies of the state, criticizing them, and the next as if they were his best buddies.

Truman and McCarthy's Attack

In fact, Truman was anything but soft on communism. Like McCarthy, he too was a tough, midwestern anticommunist. He distrusted Soviet dictator Josef Stalin the moment he met him, and he needed little persuasion to protect home and country against a foreign aggressor. Truman had fought gallantly in World War I, and he was the president who ended World War II by ordering the dropping of atomic bombs on Hiroshima and Nagasaki. He did not have to prove his patriotism or flag his anticommunist credentials, but he often acted as if he, too, were caught up in the fears generated by the Red Scare, worrying about his political reputation.

As a result, Truman sent his Justice Department on an ostentatious search for "subversive" organizations, wherever they might be. He ordered all government employees to "swear" their "loyalty" to God and country, a highly controversial order that cost him liberal support. And, on the foreign front, the president shipped military aid to Greece and Turkey, established the North Atlantic Treaty Organization (NATO), which pledged the United States to defend Western Europe against a possible Soviet assault, and launched the incomparable airlift of supplies to West Berlin, which saved the divided German city from an imminent communist takeover.

McCarthy, though, seemed unimpressed. He focused his crusade not on Berlin or Turkey but on communist "subversion and infiltration" at home, aiming his often factless assault directly at governing bigwigs and even lowly employees. McCarthy was an early adherent of what later came to be called "fake," "post-fact" or "alternative" news. It worked for him then, as it has in more recent times for another politician.

McCarthyism Is Everywhere

By the time I graduated from the City College of New York in June 1951, McCarthy was already a political powerhouse. No course in government or politics could avoid a discussion about McCarthy and McCarthyism. He charged, often with no evidence, that the government was "infested" with communists,

Marxists, and liberals (all were the same for him), who worked surreptitiously against the interests of the country. This was an earlier version of Trump's obsession with the "deep state." Everywhere, it seemed, the United States was under fierce ideological attack.

Like many other graduates, I worried about finding a job. My older brother, Bernard, then a reporter for the *New York Times*, knowing of my interest in Russian language and literature, suggested I enroll for graduate work at the Russian Research Center at Harvard University. It proved to be very practical advice. The Cold War opened many doors in the academy and in government. I studied Russian history and quickly got a job at the U.S. embassy in Moscow, which in turn led to a job at CBS and later NBC as a Moscow bureau chief, a diplomatic correspondent, and host of *Meet the Press* and numerous TV documentaries about the East-West confrontation.

Through much of my early training, McCarthyism dominated political conversation in Washington. I found the comparison of McCarthyism to communism fascinating and frightening, leading me to believe that a citizen of a democracy, sensing a move toward authoritarianism, must be willing to take action. Like a resurrected McCarthy, Trump also operates comfortably in the dark crevices of a creeping authoritarianism. The parallels were obvious—at least, so it seemed to me.

"The Finest Homes, the Finest Colleges"

On February 9, 1950, the Ohio County Women's Republican Club offered McCarthy a launching pad, an opportunity to speak at a modest Lincoln Day dinner. From Wheeling, West Virginia, the junior senator from Wisconsin would zoom into political orbit. Almost overnight, it seemed, he erupted into a national cause, riding a historic chariot from Capitol Hill to the American heartland. He became the leader of, and principal spokesman for, an extremist anticommunist crusade that threatened the very fabric of American democracy. Suddenly catapulted to unprecedented fame, though, McCarthy would, within a few years, collapse in pitiful infamy. And herein lies a truly American story of a ruthless politician shaking up the system and reveling in personal glory before running headlong into a fearless reporter and a soft-spoken Boston lawyer and one day, to his shock and surprise, finding himself friendless on Capitol Hill: no one to drink with, no podium for another thunderbolt attack on "subversive" Democrats, and, off to one side, perhaps destined for a Wisconsin museum, his historic chariot now a charred wreck.

However, when McCarthy arrived at Wheeling's Stifel Field in a Capital Airlines prop plane, he was on his best behavior, acting like a student eager to impress a professor. He went immediately to the downtown McLure Hotel, where he met his hosts. He bowed ever so slightly on being introduced to each of the women and then vigorously shook hands with the husbands who had come to hear the visitor from the nation's capital. That evening, McCarthy entertained, thrilled, and sent shivers through the 275 Republicans who filled McLure's Colonnnade ballroom. His central theme was the Cold War. "The world is split," he pronounced in somber tones, "into two vast, increasingly hostile armed camps." He paused before adding, "This is the time for the showdown," strongly implying that, in his pessimistic opinion, the "communist atheistic world" would almost certainly win.

Why would the communists win? McCarthy's reply was simplistic given the importance of the subject, but also persuasive. Many Americans were genuinely worried about the communist threat. The Soviet Union, in 1949, had successfully tested a nuclear bomb, and Mao Zedong's communists had seized power on the Chinese mainland. Less than five years after the end of World War II, the globe suddenly looked alarmingly red. The time was ripe for an anticommunist crusader, and McCarthy seemed to fill the bill.

In Wheeling, McCarthy hit the theme that he was to repeat again and again in the next few months. "The State Department," he charged, "is thoroughly infested with communists." He stared for a moment from one face to another, waiting for his message to sink in. The room went quiet, like a church in deep prayer.

Then, dramatically, he waved a sheet of paper before his congregants. "I have in my hand," he declaimed, "two-hundred-and-five cases of individuals, who would appear to be either card-carrying members or certainly loyal to the Communist Party, but who nevertheless are still helping to shape our foreign policy." Many in the audience were stunned, others puzzled. They had all heard about the threat of "communist infiltration." But 205 communists in the State Department, shaping our foreign policy!

Naming names, McCarthy pointed first to John Service, a career China specialist, who, he alleged, wanted to "torpedo our ally, Chiang Kai-shek" and "communize" China. (Service did in fact forecast a communist victory in the Chinese civil war, but that was part of an official government analysis and vastly different from McCarthy's charge that Service was working to "communize" China.) He also described Gustave Duran, an assistant secretary of state for Latin American affairs, as a "notorious international communist." His most important name, though, was Dean Acheson, the secretary of state, whom McCarthy despised and distrusted. Acheson not only protected "spies," such as Alger Hiss, who had recently been unveiled as a Soviet agent, McCarthy blustered, but he also worked to weaken the foundations of American democracy. These were Americans from "the finest homes, the finest colleges," having "the finest jobs" in the U.S. government—but, in McCarthy's view, these were also the Americans who were in active cahoots with the communists to defeat the United States and win the Cold War. He offered not a word of proof.

McCarthy then quoted "one of our outstanding historical figures" as saying: "When a great democracy is destroyed, it will not be because of enemies from without but rather because of enemies from within." He never did identify this "outstanding historical figure" but it was likely Lincoln, who once said, "If it [despotism] ever reach us, it must spring up amongst us; it cannot come from abroad." McCarthy's emphasis on "enemies from within" as being more important than "enemies from without" was in line with his attacks on Acheson and other U.S. government officials for "destroying" a "great democracy." In the process, McCarthy continued, the American people were left with an "emotional hangover and a temporary moral lapse," all desperately in need of a "spark to rekindle them."

"Happily," McCarthy chirped, "this spark has finally been supplied." And who could possibly be the one to light it? McCarthy, of course. In explaining this God-given spark, the Wisconsin senator reached the heights of absurdity when he claimed that Acheson had recently cited the Bible's Sermon on the Mount as proof that Christ "endorsed communism, high treason and betrayal of a sacred trust, a blasphemy so great that it awakened the dormant indignation of the American people." Could McCarthy possibly have believed such nonsense? Was he drunk? (He did drink a lot.) Did his usually sober-minded Republican listeners from Ohio County believe him? Acheson did once cite the Sermon on the Mount, but not at all to suggest, much less state, that Christ had "endorsed communism." (Communism, or its antecedent Marxism, was a nineteenth-century ideology, put into practice in the twentieth century. What did Christ have to do with communism?) McCarthy was a man for whom lying had become a normal means of communication. He lived in a world of his own concoctions, organized to satisfy his ego and advance his political interests. Sometimes he made absolutely no sense at all.

Example? The last sentence of his Wheeling speech.

He has lighted the spark which is resulting in a moral uprising and will end only when the whole sorry mess of twisted warped thinkers are swept from the national scene so that we may have a new birth of national honesty and decency in government.

McCarthy's syntax was so "twisted" and "warped," to use his own words against him, that it was a mission impossible to determine whether the "he" lighting "the spark" was intended in his mind to be Acheson or Christ. Since McCarthy hated Acheson, he must have meant Christ. He left the GOP women of Wheeling (and their husbands) with the farfetched impression that he, the junior senator from Wisconsin, had just arrived in West Virginia as a modern-day messiah, a special emissary from the Almighty himself, to save them and America from the scourge of communism.[1]

McCarthy got a standing ovation. Many of the women were in tears, their husbands nodding as if deep in thought, all of them expressing their gratitude to the man they might then have imagined as the Republican who would succeed Truman in the White House.

By the time McCarthy returned to Washington, he had decided to change his fantastic but eye-catching charge that he had a list of 205 communists working in the State Department. He cut it to 57 communists in the State Department before changing it to 81 communists and, by day's end, while talking to a Washington journalist, to 10 communists. The exact number was totally unimportant to McCarthy. He could have said "305 communists" or "505 communists" since he obviously had no list of whatever number. What was important was that he had broken into the news.

It did not happen instantaneously. In fact, on that memorable evening, only the local newspaper and radio station covered his speech (the station accidentally erased the only tape recording of the speech), and the Associated Press ran a 110-word story that was picked up by about two dozen newspapers around the country. But in the next week or two, McCarthy's outrageous claim that 205 communists worked in the State Department mushroomed into a national scandal, generating a wave of finger-pointing and fearmongering that came to define McCarthyism.

By May 1950, a Gallup poll reported that 85 percent of the American people had heard of McCarthy's charges, and, of those with opinions, 57 percent thought he was doing more good than harm.

"Joe Was a Demagogue, but What Could I Do?"

Years later, reporters would wonder whether McCarthy had taken them to the cleaners. Their embarrassed answer was yes, but, they then asked, what could they have done? Should they have ignored McCarthy's charges about communists "infesting" the State Department? How could they have known at the time that he was wrong? Besides, he might have been wrong about the exact number but right about the basic charge that communists had indeed "infested" the State Department. During the Red Scare, that was seen as a real possibility.

Biographer David Oshinsky wrote about this journalistic dilemma, common then as now. Covering McCarthy was "particularly frustrating." Oshinsky quoted one reporter, "My own impression was that Joe [McCarthy] was a demagogue, but what could I do? I had to report—and quote—McCarthy. How do I say in the middle of [my] story, 'This is a lie.' The press is supposed to be neutral."

The journalist David Halberstam, on his romp through *The Fifties*, his history of a transformational decade, wrote that the "real scandal" of McCarthyism was the many ways the Wisconsin senator used the press on "his traveling road show." "He knew their deadlines," Halberstam said, "when they were hungriest and needed to be fed, and when they had the least time to check out" his charges. McCarthy deliberately made announcements at 11 a.m., timed for publication in the afternoon press, and at 5 p.m. for the next day's papers.

The reporters had "little interest in reporting how careless he was or how little it all meant to him. It was news, and he was news; that was all that mattered." Willard Edwards, a political reporter for the *Chicago Tribune*, was quoted as saying, "McCarthy was a dream story. I wasn't off page one for four years."[2] For the reporter or editor who measured success by front-page exposure, this was heaven. For the senator, the front page was proof he had made it, a form of journalistic recognition of his powerhouse status in national politics.

Journalists have always had the responsibility of covering the news as it happens, as fairly as possible; only later do they have the luxury—and the responsibility—of returning to the story and double-checking it for accuracy and perspective. If journalists were blessed with hindsight, they would be more accurate and less susceptible to political manipulation. But they are not so blessed. They have to report the news, as best they can, on tight deadlines, recognizing that personal ambition and competitive pressures often compel them to report first what they should have checked more carefully. What was noteworthy, then as now, was that most of the time they get it right.

Clearly, in 1950, McCarthy played with the press, and won the day.

FIVE

"He Had a Certain Raw Wit and Charm"

FROM WHEELING, WEST VIRGINIA, Joseph McCarthy went hopscotching around the country, speaking at one Republican women's club or another, or a foreign affairs group, always pushing his central thesis—that the nation was in dire peril because of communist subversion and infiltration; that the nation was being destroyed not just by Russians but also "from within," by Americans "born with silver spoons in their mouths." Much to his delight, McCarthy attracted huge globs of attention. In this climate of unreasoning hysteria, associated with the Red Scare in the early 1950s, he had become the Pied Piper of anticommunism. He played to the fears of people, to the uncertainty many felt about their tomorrows. One result of this fear campaign was that many people in government, in academia, and in the media and entertainment lost their jobs. McCarthy succeeded in equating any left-wing sentiment with communism and then accused all liberals of being disloyal to the United States. These liberals felt—and in reality were—helpless. Distinctions in political allegiance were lost, careers damaged, lives broken.

Wherever he traveled, McCarthy, a Catholic, always attracted enthusiastic support from the Catholic Church, which at the time fully shared his passion for uprooting communists at home and fighting them abroad. The church and the senator were twinned to the strategy of keeping America safe from "communist subversion." For example, Father Edmund Walsh, the dean of Georgetown University's School of Foreign Service, who was as single-mindedly anticommunist as he was antiblack and anti-Semitic, spotted McCarthy as an appealing newcomer. The dean quickly became an active supporter and defender, and he prodded McCarthy to go for bigger fish, most especially President Truman.

Another influential supporter was Francis Cardinal Spellman of New York, often called the "Vicar of Vietnam," for his total dedication to the anticommunist cause there. The cardinal often went out of his way to praise McCarthy. Magically, money found its way from the Catholic Church in New York to McCarthy's political coffers in Wisconsin.

In addition, practical political advice and financial support came from the powerful Kennedy clan in Massachusetts, usually Democratic by political inclination but decidedly pro-McCarthy because of his Catholicism and his anticommunist crusade. The deeply conservative patriarch, Joseph Kennedy—President Franklin D. Roosevelt's former ambassador to Great Britain—was immensely impressed by the McCarthy crusade. He often invited the Wisconsin senator to the Kennedy estate on Cape Cod, and McCarthy obliged and became a frequent visitor. While there, the senator dated two of Kennedy's daughters, Patricia and Eunice. "He had a certain raw wit and charm," Eunice once remarked, "when he had not had too much to drink." Joe Kennedy provided money and valuable contacts, as did many other Bay State Catholics. He arranged for his son, Robert, to work on the senator's controversial Permanent Subcommittee on Investigations, and he encouraged another son, John, by that time a senator, to avoid voting against any McCarthy initiative or joining his Democratic colleagues in criticizing McCarthy. Amazingly, even when McCarthy ran into severe trouble in 1954, leading to his Senate censure, both John and Robert retained their friendship with the Wisconsin senator, though by then it was strained. John even managed to be absent when the vote came on McCarthy's censure, a decision that was to haunt him for years.

Kennedy's biographer, Theodore Sorenson, seeking to explain this embarrassing misstep, argued that Kennedy was in a Florida hospital suffering from a bad back and was too ill to vote. "I was in bad shape," Kennedy later said, "and I had other things on my mind."

Historian Robert Dallek followed the facts and concluded that Kennedy could easily have joined other Democrats in voting for the McCarthy censure. But he didn't. "For someone who admired courage of any kind, physical, emotional, political," Dallek wrote, "Kennedy failed the test by ducking the vote, avoiding taking a stand for reasons of political expediency, and short-term political expediency at that."

Perhaps, at the end of the day, Kennedy did not want to hurt his father, who continued to admire McCarthy, Perhaps he did not want to offend his broader Democratic constituency of Massachusetts Catholics, many of whom balanced their political sympathies by supporting Republican McCarthy and yet voting for Democrat Kennedy. Or perhaps, as he later acknowledged, he had simply made a colossal blunder.

"By the Hour" at the Carroll Arms

McCarthy, in the months following his meteoric rise to power, lived the life of the bachelor politician in Washington, which often meant retiring to the bar at the Carroll Arms Hotel on the corner of 1st and C Streets after work for a drink, or two or three, or for a rendezvous with any available lady (the Carroll Arms was known to rent rooms by the hour), or for a serious confab with a Senate colleague at the famous Quorum Club on the second floor. McCarthy spent many happy hours at the hotel. Even after a Senate subcommittee denounced his Wheeling revelations as a "fraud and a hoax," he was still welcomed at the Carroll Arms Hotel. In fact, everyone was welcomed there. It was the most popular watering hole on Capitol Hill.

A Lady from Maine Has a "Declaration of Conscience"

Though McCarthy at the time was riding a high wave of popular adoration and enjoying his moment in the sun, there was also little doubt that wisps of criticism were beginning to form on the near horizon. A number of reporters were raising questions about some of the wild charges he was hurling at prominent Americans, and on Capitol Hill a small gaggle of senators gathered in private to consider ways of controlling the seemingly uncontrollable junior senator from Wisconsin. But despite this muted criticism, very few Americans, whether reporters or senators, were courageous enough to stand up and challenge McCarthy. They were afraid he would turn his anticommunist fury on them.

Still, word began to spread in the spring of 1950 that Maine's Margaret Chase Smith, though only a freshman senator, was becoming increasingly dismayed by McCarthy's ugly politics, and she was planning to go after him. On June 1, 1950, as she headed toward the Senate chamber, speech in hand, she bumped into McCarthy on the Senate subway.

"Margaret, you look very serious," he joked. "Are you going to make a speech?"

"Yes," she shot back, "and you will not like it."

Joined by six Republican colleagues, she rose and the chamber fell to a hushed silence. "We are Republicans," she explained. "But we are Americans first." Saying she was deeply troubled by her colleague's "irresponsible words of bitterness and selfish political opportunism," she read a remarkable "Declaration of Conscience," in which she fearlessly detailed "a national feeling of fear and frustration that could result in *national suicide* and the *end of everything that we Americans hold dear*." Explaining what prompted her defiant Declaration, she ticked off four reasons: "I speak as a Republican. I speak as a woman. I speak as a United States Senator. I speak as an American." Smith was, as John Kennedy said, "a very formidable political figure."

Smith declared that the Senate, once hailed as "the greatest deliberative body in the world," had been reduced to "a forum of hate and character assassination, a "publicity platform of irresponsible sensationalism . . . a rendezvous for vilification, for selfish political gain at the sacrifice of individual reputations and national unity." She did not mention McCarthy by name, but everyone knew he was her target. The Constitution, she made clear, guaranteed not only "freedom of speech" but also "trial by jury instead of trial by accusation." She stressed that the American people were entitled to "the right to criticize, the right to hold unpopular beliefs, the right to protest, the right of independent thought"—rights, she feared, McCarthy was beginning to view with increasing hostility.

Exercising these "basic principles of Americanism" should not "cost one single American citizen his reputation nor his right to a livelihood" she proclaimed, "nor should he be in danger of losing his reputation or livelihood, merely because he happens to know someone who holds unpopular beliefs. Who of us doesn't? Otherwise none of us could call our souls our own. Otherwise thought control would have set in."

The senator from Maine had a well-deserved reputation for speaking truth to power. She said Americans were "afraid to speak their minds lest they be politically smeared as 'Communists' or 'Fascists,'" that "freedom of speech" was "not what it used to be in America," and that America was "divided" by "suspicions" spreading like "cancerous tentacles" of a "know nothing, suspect everything" approach to policy formation, leading "rapidly," in her view, to America "losing its position as leader of the world."

Toward the end of her speech, Smith bowed briefly to the demands of politics. She felt the need to level a few stinging blows at the Truman administration for "mismanaging" the affairs of state and "pitifully" failing to "provide effective leadership." But she did so, it seemed, with half a heart, saying that "as an American, I condemn a Republican 'Fascist' as much as I condemn a Democrat 'Communist.' . . . I want to see our nation recapture the strength and unity it once had when we fought the enemy instead of ourselves." If the Republicans were to win the next election, which she obviously favored, she hoped that it would not be on "the Four Horsemen of Calumny—Fear, Ignorance, Bigotry and Smear," in other words, on the back of McCarthy's unrelenting anticommunism, but rather on the basis of a proper GOP platform of lower taxes, economic expansion, and a strong military.[1]

Her colleagues, surprised by the power of her speech, applauded her courage, although many of them refused to run the risk of offending McCarthy and feared he might label them communist sympathizers or sexual perverts. McCarthy himself stomped out of the chamber and later laughingly dismissed Smith and her supporters as "Snow White and the Six Dwarfs."

Some newspapers, including the prominent political press, lavished praise on her "Declaration of Conscience." Columnist Walter Lippmann cheered her "noble declaration." Elder statesman Bernard Baruch declared that if a man had delivered the speech, "he would be the next president." *Newsweek* set its sights a bit lower, running a cover story headlined "Senator Smith: A Woman Vice-President?"

Even so, McCarthy's anticommunist crusade was still a raging prairie fire. National headlines were routinely filled with McCarthy "accusing," "branding," "charging," "defying," "demanding," or "threatening" one target or another, always on the attack, unaware, it seemed, of his obvious paucity of fact, hard information, or reliable intelligence. People, still afraid, were marching to his drumbeat.

Moreover, a few weeks after Smith's declaration, everyone's attention quickly shifted to Korea, where the North had invaded the South. President Truman responded by sending troops to the bloody peninsula. The boiling intensity of the Cold War had the ironic effect of sidelining Smith and elevating McCarthy, whose anticommunist crusade only grew wider and stronger. In 1951, proving McCarthy never forgot a slight, certainly not a stinging attack, McCarthy got his revenge on Smith, kicking her off the prized investigation subcommittee he chaired and replacing her with a rising star from California who shared his anticommunist fervor, Richard Nixon.

Time, Collier's, *Even the* Daily Worker *Speak Out*

When, later in June 1950, apparently inspired by Senator Smith's "Declaration of Conscience," *Time* magazine let loose a blistering critique of McCarthy's many obvious failings, the rampaging senator, indifferent to reality, quickly counterattacked, accusing *Time* of "twisting and distorting the facts about my fight to expose and remove Communists from government."

McCarthy always realized that, for him to continue to succeed in his crusade against communists, he needed the press, but unfortunately, he misunderstood the role of the press in a democratic society. He believed that, once he became a nationwide symbol of anticommunism, the press would praise him. Certainly print and TV would become friendly turf! McCarthy adored the headlines, and his appearances on television transformed him into a political star, in the process doing wonders for his ego and his cause. But, if by chance or design, the press coverage ever got uncomfortably critical of him or his tactics, he knew he could always accuse the offending newspaper, magazine, or network of secretly harboring communist sympathizers, assuming that his accusation would be enough to persuade the journalists to change their tone and become more positive in covering him. If necessary, McCarthy could always up the ante and attack not just the news organization's editorial policy but also its financial backers, in this way cutting into its profits and threatening its very survival.

Which is exactly what he did. On Senate stationery, lending the prestige of the U.S. Congress to his message, McCarthy sent letters to "practically all *Time* advertisers," charging that they were "unknowingly helping to pollute and poison the waterholes of information," including *Time* magazine. "It is much more important to expose a liar, a crook or a traitor, who is able to poison the streams of information flowing into a vast number of American homes," he charged, "than to expose an equally vicious crook, liar or traitor who has no magazine or newspaper outlet for his poison." He implied that *Time* advertisers, "unknowingly," were themselves liars, crooks, and traitors, who, with their financial support of *Time*, were blocking McCarthy from tending to his urgent mission of saving America from communist subversion and infiltration. In so doing, the advertisers were supporting the communist cause. His reasoning was tortured, and again he offered no proof, but his charges enthused his base of supporters.

Yet, anticipating that the "unthinking," as he labeled his critics, would surely claim that he was trying to muzzle the press, thereby striking at the heart of "freedom of the press," as guaranteed by the Constitution, McCarthy argued that "to allow a liar to hide behind the cry 'You are endangering freedom of the press' is not only ridiculous, it is dangerous." Who was the liar? Who was hiding? Neither *Time*, nor *Collier's*, nor any other magazine had ever accused McCarthy of endangering freedom of the press. As so often happened in his public proclamations, McCarthy got entangled in his own sloppy syntax and convoluted arguments, which might have confused him as much as everyone else.

A few weeks later, in Syracuse, New York, McCarthy recklessly accused the *Washington Post* of promoting the same editorial policy as the *New York Daily Worker*. They "parallel each other quite closely in editorials," he stated, without any supporting evidence. In fact, the *Post* was an independent newspaper, tilting toward a moderate editorial position on all problems, domestic or foreign, and the *Daily Worker* routinely mouthed the communist line, no matter the issue. As a senator, working in Washington, McCarthy undoubtedly read the

Washington Post every day, but the *Daily Worker* very rarely if at all.

When asked, facetiously, if he considered the staid, serious *Christian Science Monitor* to be a "left-wing smear paper," he refused to answer. "I can't answer yes or no," he replied.

On August 2, *Collier's* magazine summed up an anti-McCarthy editorial by referring back to the senator's comments about the *Washington Post* and the *Christian Science Monitor.* "Those are the statements of a man," it wrote, "who is either woefully unperceptive or wholly irresponsible. And when such a man asks that his wild-swinging attacks be accepted without question, he is, to borrow his own words, not only ridiculous but dangerous." So as not to be accused of being "another left-wing smearer," *Collier's* concluded that it was also concerned about "the real danger of communist infiltration in government" but that this danger was "too serious to be obscured and clouded by Senator McCarthy's eccentricities, exaggerations and absurdities."

Would No One Rise to Clip His Wings?

In less than a year after his Wheeling speech, McCarthy was widely seen as a major politician who placed the "danger" of "communist subversion and infiltration" near the top of the national agenda, and it was to remain there until the Republican leadership of Congress, in the fall of 1954, summoned up the courage to censure McCarthy, effectively ending his political career. What was remarkable was that so many Americans truly disliked, distrusted, and disagreed with McCarthy yet feared his fiery anticommunism so much—frightened that it could at any moment be turned on them—that they shriveled into a spineless opposition, careful about what they said, what they read, what they studied, always hoping someone else would have the courage to challenge McCarthy and denounce his unsubstantiated attacks on senior government officials and his obvious undermining of American democracy. Would no one rise to clip his wings? Even when Senator Smith and a few others did rise, it seemed to have had no effect on McCarthy's troubling and persistent ability to intimidate a nation. Thus, for a time, McCarthyism reigned "in the land of the free and the home of the brave."

How stunningly similar—spineless Republicans cowering before McCarthy in the early 1950s and today's senior Republican leadership turning a blind eye and a deaf ear to Donald Trump's unsubstantiated accusations. The parallels are powerful and disturbing.

SIX

Ike vs. McCarthy

ONE MIGHT HAVE THOUGHT that if there was one American who could clip McCarthy's wings, it would be the popular Dwight D. Eisenhower, a man of honor born and bred in the breadbasket of America, a professional soldier who rose through the ranks to become an army general and supreme allied commander during World War II. And then, in 1952, after a brief stop at Columbia University (he accepted the job there as president, even though everyone knew he was a short-timer) he moved, first, to win the Republican Party's nomination for president of the United States, and second, on election night, to clobber his Democratic opponent, the erudite, experienced governor of Illinois, Adlai Stevenson, and gain the political prize more coveted than any other in the free world. Ike became president.

Some Americans might have thought they had elected a man who, among other things, could restore domestic harmony—meaning that he would shout down or shut down the one senator who was riding the Red Scare express and running the nation into a dead end of fear and fright. They were to be painfully disappointed.

Ike decided that he would have nothing to do with McCarthy. According to his biographer, Robert J. Donovan, Ike was "disgusted" and "infuriated" by the Wisconsin senator, but he would not get into a shouting match with him. His public attitude could best be described as one of patient disdain. He would try to ignore the senator. He would outwait him, hoping the "common sense" of the American people would ultimately bring McCarthy down to earth.

Donovan noticed that Ike's live-and-let-live approach to the problem left a "discouraging void in the movement against McCarthy." Indeed, many Americans believed that McCarthyism was the single most important problem facing the nation, and for them, the president's attitude was "so unsatisfying as to be almost unendurable." Many friends pleaded with Ike to use the power of the White House pulpit to destroy McCarthy, but he would not go down that road. When his aides once urged him to attack McCarthy, Ike snapped angrily, "I will not get in the gutter with that guy." He even refused to endorse publicly what his oldest brother, Arthur, a Kansas City banker, had said of McCarthy. The senator was at the moment "the most dangerous menace to America," Arthur Eisenhower had posited, "a throwback to the Spanish Inquisition."

By attacking McCarthy directly, by name, Ike thought he would be giving McCarthy equal billing—"Ike vs. McCarthy," like a heavyweight boxing match—and he would not allow McCarthy to be seen as an equal of the president, someone who could even possibly supplant him. "He wants to be President," Ike told an aide one day. "He's the last guy in the world who'll ever get there if I have anything to say." But Ike, resorting to what scholar Fred Greenstein called the "hidden hand" approach to presidential leadership, rarely said anything critical of McCarthy in public. Not until the senator actually began to lose power in 1954 did Ike speak up, and then very carefully.

For a time, Ike's "hidden hand" notwithstanding, McCarthy was everywhere, impossible to ignore, forcing his way into the action, reaping the headlines he so craved.

For example, during the 1952 election campaign, McCarthy desperately sought Ike's support for his own reelection run in Wisconsin. Initially Ike's instinct was not to give his support, but he ended up giving it, though with minimal enthusiasm. McCarthy, always the fighter, boarded Ike's campaign train from Chicago to Milwaukee, even though he was not given a formal invitation. Along the way, he pressed Ike's speechwriters to drop a paragraph from his speech, to be delivered that evening, in part praising General George C. Marshall, who had served as Truman's secretary of state and of defense and had endured heavy doses of McCarthy criticism as a "traitor" who had abandoned China to Mao Zedong. In mid-June, the Wisconsin senator had delivered a venomous three-hour attack on the "mysterious" Marshall, describing him as part of a nefarious communist conspiracy so immense it surpassed any "such venture" in history.

Ike knew that Marshall was an extraordinary public servant, a totally dedicated patriot who had done more to advance his own career during World War II than anyone else, promoting him over other, more senior officers. Yet when the Republican governor of Wisconsin, Walter J. Kohler Jr., on welcoming Ike to Milwaukee, also urged Ike to drop his praise of Marshall, in this way echoing McCarthy's approach, Ike shamefully retreated, dropping his positive references to Marshall. Later, on leaving Milwaukee, he even, though indirectly, issued a statement of support for McCarthy, saying simply that he backed "all Republican candidates." Apparently, by not mentioning McCarthy by name, Ike felt momentarily virtuous. But where, then, reporters wanted to know, did Ike differ from McCarthy? On "method," Ike explained meekly. They both agreed, Ike replied, on the importance of eliminating "communist subversives" from government service. They disagreed on how McCarthy went about eliminating them from government service. This would not be the only time Ike backed into the shadows of ambiguous rhetoric and political obfuscation to hide his refusal to use his personal and political power to confront McCarthy and challenge his assault on American democracy.

For the first two years of Ike's presidency—applauded then and now in so many other ways, from ending the fighting in Korea to watering the seeds of economic growth—the general-turned-politician found that, in one way at least, he had failed to achieve an important goal. He could not sideline McCarthy, who always seemed to loom before him as an insurmountable, frustrating roadblock.

Early in 1954, a Gallup poll reported that close to 50 percent of the American people had a favorable impression of McCarthy. Except for Ike, he was the most popular Republican in the country. History guards its secrets until the last moment, which may explain why McCarthy in reality stood in February 1954 at the edge of his own stunning demise; but he didn't know it, nor did anyone else. Within months, he was to be stripped of his political magic by CBS's Edward R. Murrow, humiliated by a Boston lawyer named Joseph Welch in what came to be known as the Army-McCarthy hearings, robbed of the chairmanship of his once powerful investigation subcommittee, and ultimately censured by his Senate colleagues.

Like a balloon that suddenly lost air, McCarthy collapsed into the final shameful phase of his political career, looking like an alcoholic relic of an embarrassing period in American history. He died in 1957.

The Sudden, Surprising Stop to McCarthy and McCarthyism

While the Constitution establishes three branches of government—legislative, executive, judicial—it was arguably the "fourth branch," the stubborn, restless, and irascible press, led by Murrow, that pressured the legislative branch to gather its strength, harrumph a time or two, and finally topple McCarthy from power. The judicial branch watched from afar, determined to do nothing, and the executive branch, led by Ike, smiled in silent satisfaction.

What did finally topple McCarthy?

The conventional view is that the Army-McCarthy hearings, as they were called, televised over a few months, revealed the senator's dark personality, and the American people, repelled by what they saw, heard, and read, turned against him, and this, in turn, allowed Republican leaders to take a deep breath and, with a twitch of courage, finally begin to act against McCarthy.

The respected author Jon Meacham has advanced a more intriguing analysis, based in part on the judgment and experience of Franklin D. Roosevelt. "People tire of seeing the same name day after day in the important headlines of the papers," Meacham quoted Roosevelt as saying, "and the same voice night after night on radio." Even apparently if the "name" and "voice" belong to a president, people have a way of saying, "enough." For an unspecified time, they admire the name and love the voice, but then change their minds. They have seen and heard enough.[1]

To explain McCarthy's sudden collapse, Meacham also leaned on the analysis of McCarthy's devious chief counsel, Roy Cohn. The Army-McCarthy hearings were a "setback," Cohn said, but the "more fundamental reason" for McCarthy's downfall was that no "holder of high office" could "remain indefinitely at the center of controversy." The public always sought "new thrills," wrote Cohn, and eventually the senator had "nothing to offer but the same." After more than three years in the political limelight, "the surprise, the drama [associated with McCarthy], were gone."

Few knew McCarthy better than Cohn. "He acted on impulse." Cohn said. "He tended to sensationalize the evidence he had in order to draw attention to the rock bottom seriousness of the situation. He would neglect to do important homework and consequently would, on occasion, make challengeable statements. He was selling the story of America's peril. He knew he could never hope to convince anybody by delivering a dry general-accounting-office type of presentation. In consequence, he stepped up circumstances a notch or two"—which was Cohn's way of saying McCarthy lied, distorted, exaggerated, and twisted the truth. Clearly, Cohn tried to paint McCarthy in positive colors, and so he did not acknowledge that the senator's falsehoods had alarmed the American people and damaged American democracy. He and McCarthy were indissolubly linked in their reckless disregard of proper congressional and constitutional norms. Time and again, the parallel with Trump is unavoidable.

In Meacham's view, McCarthy oversold both himself and his strident anticommunist "product." His customers, the public, "tired of the pitch, and the pitchman." Like Roosevelt and Cohn, Meacham believed that the American people could accept just so much malarkey from a politician and then, at an often unremarkable moment, they rebel. Though Meacham was analyzing McCarthy, he was really thinking about Donald Trump. His belief was that just as the public ultimately tired of McCarthy, they would soon tire of Trump.

Possible, but not necessarily so. In 2018, a ruling, unprincipled demagogue has many more tools at his disposal than did McCarthy. Much has changed in American press and politics since the 1950s.

SEVEN

Senator, Meet Edward R. Murrow

EDWARD R. MURROW STOOD ALONE in American journalism in the 1940s and 1950s. There were other fine journalists, of course, many of whom also covered World War II and presidential campaigns in the United States, but none left so inspirational a legacy or had so major an impact. He was unique because he was first to bring the drama and surprise of an ever-changing world directly into American homes, starting in 1937 with what his colleague, William L. Shirer, called "this newfangled radio broadcasting business" and then in postwar America with the mind-blowing success of TV news. What people heard and saw, they believed, in large part because Murrow was the messenger—he was trusted. "His facts were solid, his scope thorough, his analysis on target," wrote his biographer, Bob Edwards, "and his principles uncompromised." He was America's "foremost broadcast journalist."

On March 9, 1954, Murrow took on the senator from Wisconsin, who had struck fear into the hearts of so many Americans. In his CBS News evening program *See It Now*, Murrow showed the American people that Joseph McCarthy was nothing more than a thin skeleton of lies and phony bluster, certainly no one to fear. His program was a scathing indictment of a political fraud. Soon thereafter, also on network television, the Senate's Army-McCarthy hearings opened, and they were an instant hit, further exposing McCarthy's bullying and fearmongering. Even his supporters began to ask questions. Only then did his Republican colleagues take him on. Up to that point, most of them—aside from Senator Margaret Chase Smith—had choked at the thought of challenging McCarthy. But let there be no mistake: the unraveling of McCarthy began with Murrow's historic broadcast.

From Guilford County to New York City

Murrow was an American original. He was born in April 1908, in Guilford County, North Carolina, the youngest of four sons. Ethel and Roscoe Murrow, his parents, lived in a log cabin with no electricity, no plumbing, and no heat except for a small wood-burning stove. When Murrow was five, his family moved cross-country to Blanchard, a small town in Washington thirty miles from the Canadian border. Life was tough. His father taught him how to shoot. His mother taught him to read aloud one chapter from the Bible every night.

After graduating from high school, Murrow worked for a year at a nearby logging camp and then, in 1926, enrolled in Washington State College. He majored in speech, mastered the classics, led his fraternity, played basketball, served as an ROTC cadet colonel, and won election not only as president of the student body but also as head of the Pacific Student Presidents Association.

In 1929, he attended the annual convention of the National Student Federation of America, where he delivered a stirring speech urging his colleagues to become more interested in national and global affairs than in "fraternities, football and fun." Much to his surprise, Murrow was elected the federation's new president.

After graduation in 1930, as the world (and the United States) slumped into the Great Depression, Murrow moved to New York City, where he ran the Student Federation's national office. He focused on higher education. Journalism was still a profession over the horizon. Within a few months he was in Europe, attending a meeting of the Confederation Internationale des Etudiants in Brussels. Little was accomplished because, like their countries, the delegates were divided over the hotly debated subject of German representation. Murrow argued that young Germans should not have to bear the World War I sins of their fathers—they should be invited. Though he lost the argument, he won the hearts of the delegates, who urged him to be their new president. Murrow declined, returning to New York, where he plunged into fundraising and public relations for the Student Federation. He persuaded the *New York Times* to publish its student polls and, more important, in light of where he would eventually find his fame, he created and coproduced the *University of the Air* series for the two-year-old Columbia Broadcasting System (CBS), his foot in the door of the new world of broadcasting.

Murrow was now on the move. In 1932 he joined Stephan Duggan at the Institute of International Education, part of the Carnegie Endowment. Duggan enjoyed a wide range of contacts in politics, business, and education, and Murrow got to meet many of them, including New York governor Franklin

Roosevelt, who was, among other things, gearing up to run for president.

At Duggan's suggestion, Murrow returned to Europe. He was driven and young (twenty-four), and, more than anything, he wanted to turn higher education into a vehicle for peaceful exchanges among nations, a way of heading off the confrontation he saw developing in Europe. His assignment was, whenever possible, to arrange exchange programs, even with the Soviet Union, and then to evaluate the many scholars, writers, and musicians seeking invitations to lecture and perform in the United States. It was a formidable task, and the program with Moscow backfired when Murrow lost control of it. Two years later, Hearst carried a story suggesting unfairly that the Institute of International Education had been running a kind of communist propaganda school in Moscow. McCarthy would later use the story in an effort to smear Murrow.

In 1933, after Adolf Hitler's Nazis seized control of Germany and began purging universities, burning books, and banishing Jews, Duggan, Murrow, and the heads of twenty-one American colleges formed the Emergency Committee in Aid of Displaced German Scholars. Murrow, an assistant to Duggan and still president of the National Student Federation of America, was given the job of running the committee. Funding came from the Rockefeller and Carnegie Foundations. For the next few years, Murrow worked tirelessly, trying to find jobs in America for scholars who could no longer work in Germany. He succeeded in relocating hundreds of them, including Paul Tillich, Martin Buber, Thomas Mann, Felix Bloch, and Hans Morgenthau. It was, he later said, "the most satisfying thing I ever did in my life." Throughout this period, Murrow thought of himself as an educator, though he was at the time only one or two steps away from becoming the most consequential journalist of his time.

Inventing Radio News while Covering World War II

Murrow's first step was to join CBS in September 1935 as director of talks, a new position seemingly crafted for his special skills and experience. He was not to broadcast; he was to arrange programs. With network resources behind him, he covered the U.S. election campaign, the abdication of Britain's King Edward VIII, Mussolini's war in Ethiopia, and, of course, Hitler's upheaval in Germany. In his new job, he did well. On one occasion, after an office Christmas party, Murrow pleaded with CBS's top broadcaster, Robert Trout, to allow him to do the evening newscast. Murrow yearned for the experience. Reluctantly, Trout yielded, and Murrow did his broadcast—and did it flawlessly. It was a *Wow!* moment, which Murrow was to cherish for years.

He took his second step on April Fool's Day in 1937, one year before Hitler annexed Austria in the historic Anschluss that effectively started World War II. With his wife, Janet, at his side, Murrow sailed to England, where he was to produce "jolly" programs about flower shows and the British Open, while the British government, reflecting the mood of much of the rest of Europe, embraced appeasement as its policy toward Hitler's militarization of Germany. Sensing the imminence of war, Murrow hired William L. Shirer, an experienced newspaperman, to help him and CBS cover the fast-moving developments in Europe, even though New York still favored sports programs and children's choirs over news.

On March 9, 1938, Nazi troops marched into Austria. Three days later, Shirer, in his first radio report, described how Germany annexed Austria. It was hardly a CBS exclusive, and no one in New York really liked Shirer's voice, but it triggered a series of decisions that inaugurated a new era in broadcast news. Whether it was Murrow's idea or CBS president

William Paley's (the debate continued for years, unresolved), CBS decided to do a quick half-hour roundup of the news from different locations in Europe, and it would be broadcast live on Sunday evening, March 13. Shirer and a member of Parliament would be in London, Murrow in Vienna, along with newspaper reporters in Paris, Berlin, and Rome. Such a broadcast had never been attempted before. New York asked Shirer, "Can you and Murrow do it?" Shirer answered yes, and hung up, later admitting he had no idea how it would or could be done. But it was, for a reporter, breathtakingly exciting. "Instantaneous transmission of news from the reporter to the listener, in his living room, of the event itself," Shirer explained, "so that the listener could follow it just as it happened . . . was utterly new."

The broadcast was an immediate success, and CBS ordered another roundup for the following night. Can you do it? New York again wanted to know. "No problem," replied Shirer, excited by the challenge. And so was born what today is taken for granted—live broadcasts from different corners of the globe, journalists assigned to cover stories and provide reports and analysis, and the public tuned into breaking news that affects their lives. It took only a few roundups for CBS to realize that it had stumbled on more than just a new way of broadcasting and analyzing the news; it had also discovered, in Edwards's words, "the patron saint and first great star" of broadcast news.

Murrow proved to be a natural: he was smart, he was ambitious, and he felt he had an urgent job to do—to tell the American people that a new evil had descended upon Europe. And that something had to be done about it!

The Murrow Boys and the Blitz

Most reporters get started covering local fires, sports, or City Hall. Murrow got started covering the outbreak of World War II. Operating out of London, he hired a team of experienced reporters, later dubbed the "Murrow Boys." Shirer returned to Berlin. Thomas Grandin and Eric Sevareid were hired in Paris, Mary Marvin Breckinridge in Amsterdam, and then Cecil Brown in Rome, Larry LeSueur in London, and Winston Burdett in Oslo. Charles Collingwood and Howard K. Smith later joined the team.

For every reporter based in Europe, the story in 1938 was Hitler's aggression against the Sudetenland in Czechoslovakia, in effect accomplished with the acquiescence of British Prime Minister Neville Chamberlain. That was followed on September 1, 1939, by Germany's invasion of Poland, opening another European war that would quickly spread across the world and cost tens of millions of lives.

The overwhelming question in London was whether Britain would again acquiesce, as it had with the Sudetenland, or whether it would finally stand up to Germany. Murrow felt that this time, Britain would, however reluctantly, support Poland, even if that meant going to war against Germany, a position he expressed in a broadcast. He was now being heard regularly on CBS Radio. Indeed, when Americans were now listening to news about the spreading conflict in Europe, they were listening to Murrow or his Boys. "Am I right on this?" Murrow anxiously asked his British censor before going on air. "I have to be right." Britain declared war on Germany, and the Battle for Britain began. It was the story that launched Murrow's extraordinary career.

By the summer of 1940, Hitler had already occupied most of Europe, except for the Soviet Union in the east and Great

Britain in the west. On August 24, Germany began a relentless bombing campaign of Great Britain, the so-called Blitz. It was seen as a prelude to a Nazi invasion, which, as it turned out, never happened. Night after night, German planes bombed a widening range of targets, from the loading docks in East London, teeming with workers, to the elite in Buckingham Palace. Big Ben was not spared, nor was Parliament. Tens of thousands of people were killed.

Murrow's coverage of the Blitz was urgent and unprecedented. He would switch from analyzing Prime Minister Winston Churchill's wartime speeches and strategy to describing a simple flower shop, a grocery, or a restaurant that had been bombed and left in smoking, bloody ruins. He was endlessly curious, walking the streets of London, night or day, nothing so seemingly insignificant as to be ignored, every face, blast, or random chat a possible story. Murrow's coverage of the Blitz may have been radio's finest hour.

One night he did a broadcast called "London after Dark." He left the comfortable surroundings of his studio and went to the St. Martin-in-the-Fields church near Trafalgar Square. Nearby was an air raid shelter. There was no panic as another air raid began. But how to convey the fact that there was no panic? That the British were tough, their spirit unflagging? Murrow came up with the simple idea of holding his microphone close to the ground, picking up the sounds of people walking unhurriedly into the shelter, "like ghosts shod with steel shoes," he said.

On another night, he climbed to a rooftop near BBC headquarters so he could "hear" London under air attack: the whistling sound of bombs and then the explosions; police and wardens shouting warnings, urging care; skylines described in rich detail, presumably based on notes he had taken on an earlier visit: "that faint-red, angry snap of antiaircraft bursts against the steel blue sky . . . the sound of guns off in the distance, very faintly, like someone kicking a tub . . . four search lights reach up, disappear in the light of a three quarter moon." Mostly Murrow ad-libbed, using crisp words to paint portraits of a bombing attack for listeners who were an ocean away and still at peace.

When he wanted to describe the stiff-upper-lip determination of the British people not only to survive the German bombing but to win the war, he again relied on his verbal paint brush, his words. "Today . . . I decided to have a haircut. The windows of the barbershop were gone, but the Italian barber was still doing business. 'Someday,' he said, 'we smile again, but the food—it doesn't taste so good since being bombed.' I went to another shop to buy some flashlight batteries. The clerk said, 'You needn't buy so many. We'll have enough for the whole winter.' But I said, 'What if you aren't here?' There were buildings down in that street, and he replied, 'Of course, we'll be here. We've been in business here for a hundred and fifty years.'"

Everyone at the White House listened to Murrow's broadcasts, and in January 1941 President Roosevelt's special envoy, Harry Hopkins, flew to London, among other things to see Murrow, who thought he was about to get an exclusive interview. In fact, Hopkins wanted to interview Murrow. Hopkins had heard his almost daily broadcasts and wanted to get the reporter's gut opinion about whether Britain, essentially fighting alone, could survive. "Yes" was Murrow's unqualified response. Three months later, Congress passed the Lend-Lease Act, officially ending America's stated neutrality in the war. Privately, Churchill gave full credit to Murrow's reports. So did the poet Archibald MacLeish, who complimented the broadcaster for helping crush the isolationism then still strong in many parts of the United States. "You have destroyed the superstition that what is done beyond three thousand miles of water is not really done at all," he said. "There were some people in this country who did not want the people of America to hear the things you had to say."

With each broadcast, Murrow was not only informing the American people but also enriching a new field of journalism. But he was not satisfied. He also wanted to cover the British bombing of Berlin. He finally got his chance on December 2, 1943. Before the war ended, he was to fly on twenty-four other combat missions.

In that first mission, in a Lancaster bomber code-named *D for Dog,* Murrow broadcast a long report on the quiet determination and professionalism of the Royal Air Force, especially his pilot, a "big Canadian with a slow, easy grin." Phrases from this award-winning report have been etched into the history of radio news. "A half hour before takeoff, the skies are dead, silent and expectant. . . . The flak looked like a cigarette lighter in a dark room—one that won't light. Sparks but no flame . . . the clouds below us were white, and we were black. D-Dog seemed like a black bug on a white sheet. . . . By this time we were about thirty miles from our target area in Berlin. . . . The sky ahead was lit up by bright yellow flares. . . . I was thrown to the other side of the cockpit, and there below were more incendiaries, glowing white and then turning red. The cookies—the four-thousand-pound high explosives— were bursting below like great sunflowers gone mad. . . . And I was very frightened. . . . All men would be brave if only they could leave their stomachs at home. . . . Then another plane in flames, but no one could tell whether it was ours or theirs. . . . Berlin was a kind of orchestrated hell, a terrible symphony of light and flame. . . . Men die in the sky while others are roasted alive in their cellars. . . . In about thirty five minutes, [Berlin] was hit with about three times the amount of stuff that ever came down on London in a night-long blitz. This is a calculated, remorseless campaign of destruction."

Murrow, throughout the war, was deeply troubled by Hitler's violent anti-Semitism. He was certainly among the first reporters to report on the "Final Solution," Hitler's decision to kill millions of European Jews—all of them, if he could. On December 13, 1942, well before most Americans had ever heard of Hitler's plan to annihilate the Jewish people, Murrow broadcast this report: "One is almost stunned into silence by some of the information reaching London," he said. "Some of it is months old, but it's eyewitness stuff supported by a wealth of detail and vouched for by responsible governments. . . . Millions of human beings, most of them Jews, are being gathered up with ruthless efficiency and murdered . . . a picture of mass murder and moral depravity unequaled in the history of the world."

Most of Murrow's wartime broadcasts attracted wide attention. But probably not that one. Few in America seemed to care about the plight of European Jews. On April 15, 1945, as the war was coming to a close, Murrow visited Buchenwald, a Nazi concentration camp recently liberated by American forces. He was so overwhelmed by the horror of what he saw that he wrote nothing about it for three days. He could not find the right words. But then he did. "If you are at lunch, or if you have no appetite to hear what Germans have done," he said, finally, after agonizing deliberation, "now is a good time to switch off the radio."

Murrow described a barracks, which had once stabled 80 horses. Twelve hundred men now lived there, "five to a bunk." They tried to "lift me to their shoulders. They were too weak.

Many of them could not get out of bed." He stopped at a hospital, where 200 people had died the day before. He looked into a garage. "There were two rows of bodies, stacked up like cordwood. They were thin and very white. Some of the bodies were terribly bruised, though there seemed to be little flesh to bruise. Some had been shot through the head, but they bled very little. All except two were naked."

He concluded: "Most of the men and boys had died of starvation; they had not been executed. But the manner of death seemed unimportant. Murder had been done at Buchenwald." Then, with a special poignancy, he closed, "If I've offended you by this rather mild account of Buchenwald, I'm not in the least bit sorry."

Roosevelt had died on April 15, the same day as Murrow's visit to Buchenwald. Those whom Murrow had met at this death camp praised and blessed Roosevelt, though at the time none knew of his death. Churchill, with tears in his eyes, had once told Murrow in 1941, "One day the world and history will recognize and acknowledge what it owes your president." Murrow saw the depth of that gratitude in the eyes of those who had somehow survived Buchenwald. "If there be a better epitaph," he said, "history does not record it."

Murrow Becomes Edward R. Murrow

When the war in Europe finally ended, Murrow spent more time remembering its cost in dreams shattered and lives lost than in expressing his hope for a bright and promising tomorrow. His broadcasts kept returning to "schoolboys" who grew up to be "soldiers," "timid, cautious, careful men and women who turned into heroes," "hundreds of thousands" who "starved" or were "butchered," and, throughout the Battle of Britain, "one disaster after another." "This coming winter," he predicted, "will be the worst that Europe has ever seen. There will be cold and famine and pestilence and despair and degradation."

If listeners thought in the aftermath of the war that they would be hearing cheerful, optimistic reports from Murrow, they were wrong. He was, of course, by now a fabled storyteller who could enchant his audiences with sparkling tales, studded with informative quotes from an Eisenhower or a Churchill, but he was also given to long bouts of silence and depression, when he would ignore family and friends, even his microphone. For, though Murrow had much to be grateful for—his family secure, Nazis defeated, and his journalistic career in skyrocketing ascendency—he still could not shake the horrors of what he had seen and heard during the war. They were always to stand guard near him, like gloomy columns of dark gray memories refusing to give him peace. Hitlerism, he had come to realize, had sprouted up, after all, in Germany, a supposedly civilized country in the heart of Europe. Millions had been systematically slaughtered solely because they were Jews. Millions of others because they happened to be standing in the way of the Third Reich. Murrow had then concluded, very reluctantly, that evil, a kind of cold, raw evil, could arise anywhere, even in a flourishing democracy such as the United States. He came to believe that it was the responsibility of every citizen, most especially the journalist, to stand up and confront this evil, wherever it emerged—and defeat it. The evil posed by McCarthyism was not yet on Murrow's immediate horizon, but it was not far off.

EIGHT

From the War in Europe to the War in America

FOR A RELATIVELY BRIEF TIME after the war, Murrow yielded to pleas from CBS head William Paley and returned to New York to become a network executive at CBS, responsible for news and public affairs. He played this role well enough but with little enthusiasm, and on July 19, 1947, he resigned, happy once again to return to the rank of "reporter first class."

Two months later, on September 29, he began the next phase of his career. The anticommunist Red Scare was the dominant story of the day. It called for the best in Murrow, and he rarely disappointed his listeners. But it also challenged him profoundly, leaving high points of professional pride and accomplishment mixed with periods of gloomy disappointment about CBS—and the broadcast business in general. For, on that special evening, Murrow launched a new fifteen-minute nightly news radio program, appropriately called *Edward R. Murrow with the News*. It was to run for twelve years, a long time in radio, and it quickly became the most authoritative broadcast news program in the business—and so recognized by everyone. It was also to become his favorite means of communicating with the public.

The program was divided into two parts—nine minutes of hard news, domestic and foreign, followed by a two- to three-minute commentary on the news.[1] Naturally, one recurring theme was the Cold War. The split between East and West was forcing nations and peoples to choose sides. In the United States, it eventually spawned McCarthyism, a political phenomenon that Murrow instinctively deplored. It was his courageous battle against McCarthyism that ultimately defined Murrow's career, and it started even before he had a chance to pin his favorite placard to the wall behind his desk. It read: "If I had more time, I'd write you a shorter letter." It was signed "Cicero."

Zeroing In on McCarthy

Later, in 1947, Murrow was alerted to a hearing of the House Un-American Activities Committee that focused on alleged communist influence in Hollywood. He listened and decided on the spot to devote his October 27 broadcast to this story. He was concerned that the concept of dissent was being wrongly equated with disloyalty, and, in the constrained political environment created by McCarthyism, this was dangerous. Interestingly, Murrow noted that every committee member seemed eager to prove he was more anticommunist than his colleagues, more adept at discovering hidden threats to the security of the nation. Any suggestion, no matter how faint, of communist, Marxist, or leftist sympathies was automatically enlarged into disloyalty to the state, and the actor or producer or writer was blackballed, making employment in Hollywood problematic—and impossible for some.

In his commentary that evening, Murrow left no doubt of his concerns. Congress, he said, usually investigated "what individuals . . . have or have not done, rather than what individuals think." Murrow then cut to the heart of the controversy. "The right of dissent—or, if you prefer, the right to be wrong—is surely fundamental to the existence of a democratic society. That's the right that went first in every nation that stumbled down the road to totalitarianism." He ended by quoting from none other than Adolf Hitler. "The great strength of the totalitarian state," the dictator said, "is that it will force those who fear it to imitate it." No one who had heard Murrow's broadcasts from Europe toward the end of the war would have been surprised by his defense of political dissent and his liberal interpretation of freedom in a democratic society. Hitler had proven Murrow's point. Democracy would fail, and totalitarianism succeed, if the right of a free people to differ from their government, and from one another, was ever sacrificed. Murrow's epic struggle with what would become known as McCarthyism was thus joined.

In 1948, both NBC and CBS started broadcasting fifteen-minute nightly news programs on television. Murrow could have anchored CBS's but declined the honor, partly because he did not yet appreciate the power of television and partly because he enjoyed the freedom of running his own little broadcasting empire. He did cover the political conventions as a floor reporter that summer, but devoted most of his time to his nightly radio program.

A year later, he introduced a new radio series called *This I*

Believe, in which prominent people such as Eleanor Roosevelt, Thomas Mann, and Helen Hayes were invited to lay out their personal philosophies. The series was so successful it was syndicated in eighty-five newspapers, rebroadcast by the Voice of America, and anthologized in two books.

More satisfying for Murrow, CBS allowed him to gather his foreign correspondents in New York for a televised year-end discussion on the state of the world, another very successful venture. People could now "see" the voice they knew primarily from radio. Murrow loved serving as moderator. "Years of Crisis" reminded him of the wide-ranging conversations with his bar buddies that he used to enjoy during the war.

Less satisfying for Murrow was the inescapable fact that McCarthyism was beginning to show its ugly head in the CBS newsroom. Sponsors objected when Murrow criticized Senator Joseph McCarthy, and his criticism prompted letters of outrage from angry pro-McCarthy listeners (also customers), who argued that journalists ought to keep their opinions to themselves. In theory, Murrow understood the objections of sponsors such as Campbell Soup Company, but as a journalist, he felt he had a professional obligation to point out that the senator's often wild attacks on senior government officials were accompanied by no supporting evidence, and they recklessly and needlessly damaged reputations. Campbell Soup admired Murrow but cherished its bottom line even more and pulled its sponsorship of his nightly radio program in June 1950.

At the same time, a book called *Red Channels*, published by American Business Consultants, Inc., listed the names of 151 network personalities with suspect "affiliations." Among them were several CBS employees, including two of Murrow's Boys. Howard K. Smith and Alexander Kendrick did not lose their jobs—probably because they were Murrow's Boys—but others did. Like many of McCarthy's attacks, *Red Channels* provided little to no evidence. It was the brainchild of three former FBI agents, who took it upon themselves to decide who was a security risk and who was not, and many companies paid them for this pseudo-clearance. After a while, CBS dropped the services of Red Channels but in its place set up its own security operation, the only network to do so. It was run by attorney Daniel O'Shea, who was given the power to determine who, at CBS, was deemed "loyal." He required every CBS employee to sign a loyalty oath. Many reporters looked to Murrow. What would he do? "I'll sign it, and so will you" was his surprising reply. Murrow had apparently decided that this was not the right issue on which to take his stand, which baffled some of his colleagues. Even during the Korean War, when one of his own commentaries, critical of American military strategy, was killed by CBS's top brass, he protested but did not quit. Paley had appealed to him and other senior correspondents to understand that the McCarthy challenge to the network was real; that CBS was no longer a small family business but was now a corporation seeking to diversify into other interests besides broadcasting; and that it had to turn a profit and honor its financial obligations to its stockholders. Murrow was still a very valued asset, still a close friend, but, Paley stressed, there was now a business to be run, and the basic interests of the business would on occasion take precedence over Murrow's more lofty goals of news reporting.

The Weaponizing of See It Now

Enter Fred Friendly, born in New York City with the Middle European–sounding name of Ferdinand Friendly Wachenheimer. By the time he joined CBS in 1950 to help Murrow produce a weekly radio newsmagazine called *Hear It Now*, Ferdinand was reduced to Fred, Friendly remained Friendly, and Wachenheimer was dropped into the ash can of history. Fred Friendly was a big brash bear of a man who barked orders, rarely slept, and was known to wake up reporters in the middle of the night to remind them to call him in the morning. He seemed to believe that each of the day's twenty-four hours was to be used as if there would never be another twenty-four hours. The newsmagazine lasted only six months, when it was transformed into *See It Now*, its twin on television, where it starred for years.

The first broadcast was an editorial and technological marvel. Whereas the *CBS Evening News* was fifteen minutes in length, thin in news content and primitive in visual presentation, *See It Now* was thirty minutes in length, rich and up-to-the-minute in content, and innovative and imaginative in visual presentation. It premiered on November 18, 1951. Murrow sat in the control room of Studio 41 in New York, surrounded by the tools of the new trade: cameras, lights, monitors and the control panel run by a young director named Don Hewitt. On cue, as the program opened, was a live shot of New York Harbor on one of the studio monitors, and, on another monitor, a live shot of the Golden Gate Bridge in San Francisco. A week or two earlier, this live split-screen vision of America's two great ports, separated by 3,000 miles, would have been technologically impossible. But now it had happened, along with other shots of Paris, London, Washington, and the war in Korea.

The program explored disarmament, politics in America, and a Churchill speech.

The critics raved about the new program. "It's been a long time a-comin," said one, "but we're beginning to *See It Now.*" As he had with radio news, so too now with television news: Murrow introduced a new way of reporting the news, always with an eye toward visual appeal and an ear for quality reporting and analysis. Again he proved himself to be special—with the help of Fred Friendly, special indeed. Each complemented the other, both demanding professional excellence. Ahead, they knew, was the monster challenge of McCarthyism. How would Murrow and Friendly cover it? Murrow realized that one day he would have to do a major report on McCarthy, but not yet. He believed the junior senator from Wisconsin represented a threat to American democracy. After reporting on Hitler's aggression in Europe, which led to the deadliest war in modern history, Murrow felt a powerful obligation to the American people to cover McCarthy diligently and fearlessly—not because he feared McCarthyism would lead overnight to a form of American fascism but because he feared that in time it might. For the next three years, he and Friendly followed McCarthy's every word and move, waiting for the right moment to broadcast their major report on McCarthy.

For example, a month after *See It Now*'s debut, Murrow and Friendly, who had earlier referred to themselves as "an old team trying to learn a new trade," noticed that McCarthy often whined about how the press "kicked [him] around and bullwhipped" him. Clearly, his complaints were aimed at generating an antipress, anti-elitist sentiment among his supporters. Murrow and Friendly had this all on film after watching hours of congressional testimony. They could see that it was McCarthy who did the bullwhipping, not the other way around. They decided, to prove their point, that they would collect film of McCarthy whining about the "unfair" press and then film of McCarthy harassing and humiliating his witnesses, connect the two sequences, and in this way show that it was McCarthy who lied about who was "bullwhipping" whom. It was to be self-incrimination by film, a TV technique that came to be associated with a Friendly-produced, Murrow-anchored critique. Obviously, the Wisconsin senator did not appreciate their new, facile use of film. If he, like Nixon, kept a secret "enemies list," Murrow and Friendly would certainly have been on it.

Another McCarthy story caught Murrow's eye in early 1952, an election year. The young, wealthy senator from Connecticut, William Benton, who had made his millions selling ads and publishing the *Encyclopaedia Britannica*, had attacked McCarthy's "despicable," "irresponsible" assault on the State Department and called on the Senate to censure him. He was a rookie senator and unlikely to get his way. But McCarthy, never one to use few words when many would accomplish the same end, then went on a rampage against Benton, calling him a "mental midget" and "clever propagandist," whose Democratic Party stood for "government of, by and for Communists, crooks and cronies."

Once again Murrow thought McCarthy had crossed a line of decency and decorum, in the process damaging American democracy. He invited McCarthy to do an interview on his *See It Now* program. McCarthy, always eager for TV time, accepted. A three-minute interview, no more, Murrow insisted. McCarthy nodded, apparently in agreement, but, once the interview began, not even Murrow could keep him on time. McCarthy ignored Murrow's questions and used his precious time on camera to rip into Benton. McCarthy dominated the interview—and the program. Murrow learned a lesson: avoid interviewing McCarthy; let him incriminate himself.

The following week, Murrow read a transcript of his interview with McCarthy on air, pointing out the senator's half-truths and outright lies, and then, for the rest of the program, interviewed Benton about McCarthy's tactics. Though Murrow felt good about the program, it proved to be a Pyrrhic victory. Benton lost his bid for reelection. McCarthy, riding Ike's coattails, won his.

The Interlude of Person to Person

"Edward R. Murrow" was an expanding enterprise. He did his nightly radio newscast and his weekly *See It Now* newsmagazine, and, on October 2, 1953, he launched a second weekly television program called *Person to Person*. His two radio writers, Jesse Zousmer and Johnny Aaron, had come up with the idea that if Murrow, sitting in a studio in New York, visited the homes of celebrities, wherever they happened to live, and engaged in light conversation about their lives, their careers, their prospects, it would result in a successful program. It was a frothy proposal, with a handsome potential for ratings and profit, and Murrow bought into the idea. No one was really surprised when the new program took off like a rocket—it was a ratings bonanza, and it made a lot of money. But many were surprised that Murrow would agree to host it. It wasn't his thing. Murrow had his reasons, though. He hoped *Person to Person* would help boost *See It Now*'s ratings, and, equally important, ease Paley's concerns about the controversy generally ignited by his coverage of McCarthy. In addition, by hosting

Person to Person, Murrow hoped that he was building a ratings distraction from his *See It Now* focus on McCarthy, who, for Murrow, always represented a flashing yellow light of danger to American democracy. He wanted to prevent what happened in Europe in the 1930s from happening in the United States in the 1950s.

Murrow Begins the Toppling of McCarthy

Everyone at CBS knew that Murrow would soon do a major report on McCarthy. Every week, Friendly would ask Murrow, "Is this it? Is this the week?" And Murrow, cigarette in hand, brows knitted in a question mark, would reply, "Not yet. Not quite yet." But on October 20, 1953, Murrow did a story about a young lieutenant in the Air Force Reserve that led directly to his showdown with McCarthy. It was a story about a classic case of guilt by association, and it symbolized the trembling fear and uncertainty the McCarthy era had engendered.

Murrow enjoyed reading out-of-town newspapers, and one day, in a Detroit paper, he read a story about Milo Radulovich, a senior at the University of Michigan, who, after eight years of active duty in the Air Force, was suddenly being classified as a "security risk" because of his close association with "communists or communist-sympathizers." His association, as it turned out, was with his father and sister—his father for reading a "subversive" newspaper and his sister for engaging in "questionable" activities, namely, walking a picket line. The Air Force requested Radulovich's resignation, even though it stressed that his own "loyalty" was not in question. Radulovich refused, stating as a simple unassailable fact that he would not stop seeing his father and sister. They were family. In any case, he went on, the "subversive" newspaper his father was reading was pro-Tito (the independent-minded leader of Yugoslavia), meaning anti-Soviet, and his sister's political beliefs were her own personal affair and, whatever they were, had nothing to do with him.

What was remarkable was that, during Radulovich's hearing, the Air Force never produced a single witness, and the evidence of his supposed "association" with communists was kept in a sealed envelope that was never opened. In his defense, Radulovich admitted he could have resigned quietly and avoided a hearing, but he felt he would then be left with the stigma of "security risk," jeopardizing his chances for later employment. He wanted a fair trial with evidence openly presented and witnesses cross-examined, a trial that could ultimately clear him. In addition, as a matter of family loyalty, he declared that he would not denounce his father and sister, as the Air Force had suggested he do, no matter what happened to him.

Murrow closed his program with a commentary that could easily have passed as an editorial. It was clearly his opinion. "We believe that the son shall not bear the iniquity of the father," pronounced Murrow, "even though that iniquity be proved, and in this case, it was not. . . . Whatever happens in the whole area of the relationship between the individual and the state, we do it ourselves. It cannot be blamed upon Malenkov [Georgy Malenkov, Stalin's immediate successor] or Mao Zedong, or even our allies. And it seems to us that that is a subject that should be argued about endlessly."

In the blunt outspokenness of his commentary, or editorial, Murrow appeared to have broken new ground, at least on television. He had, in fact, been similarly outspoken in many of his radio commentaries, but few people noticed them. Critic Jack

Gould, writing in the *New York Times*, said he thought this was the "first time" that a network and a sponsor had ever allowed a "vigorous editorial." They had definitely allowed it, but they did not approve of it. Neither paid for the promotional ad that ran in the *New York Times* that morning. Murrow and Friendly paid for it, $1,500 out of their own pockets.

But it was worth it. Five weeks later, the secretary of the Air Force appeared on *See It Now* to announce that Radulovich could, if he wished, retain his commission, and his father and sister would no longer be regarded as "security risks." There was little doubt that Murrow's program had raised serious questions about the Air Force's decisions and forced a change in its judgment of Lieutenant Radulovich.

Though the focus of the program was, it seemed, on a reserve lieutenant with a funny name, it was really on McCarthy and the pernicious impact his antics were having on Americans. It was therefore no accident that a few weeks later one of McCarthy's investigators, a cashiered FBI agent named Don Surine, spotted Joe Wershba, one of Murrow's reporters, outside a Senate hearing, and asked, "Hey, Joe, what's this Radwich junk you putting out?," an obvious reference to the Radulovich program. When Wershba did not answer immediately, Surine continued, with a pointed poke in his ribs, "What would you say if I told you Murrow was on the Soviet payroll in 1934?" From his briefcase, he extracted a photostat of the front page of the *Pittsburgh Sun-Telegraph*, a Hearst newspaper, from nineteen years before. It was about the Institute of International Education, where Murrow had worked for a few years, and a headline read, "American Professors, Trained by Soviet, Teach in US Schools." Surine told Wershba that this arrangement was the work of VOKS, the Soviet agency for cultural relations with foreign countries, and this made Murrow part of a "Moscow conspiracy." He quickly added that he was not accusing Murrow of being a communist, but he left Wershba with one of McCarthy's favorite aphorisms, "If it walks like a duck and talks like a duck, it must be a duck." The implication was clear: McCarthy was sending Murrow a warning that if he continued with "this Radwich junk," then his past "communist affiliations" would be exposed.

McCarthy misread Murrow. When Wershba delivered McCarthy's warning and the photostat of the *Sun-Telegraph*, Murrow, ill with a cold that day, said, "Oh, so that's what they've got." He ordered his staff to put their preparations for the major report on McCarthy into high gear. He remembered what he had told a friend only a day before. "The only thing that counts is the right to know, to speak, to think— that, and the sanctity of the courts. Otherwise, it's not America." Murrow's definition of America was the relevance of the First Amendment and the sanctity of the courts. Murrow was intent on proving the vital importance of the press, and he was not alone. Columnists Walter Lippmann, Joseph and Stuart Alsop, Drew Pearson, cartoonist Herblock, Elmer Davis, and Edward P. Morgan joined in the anti-McCarthy parade, but it was Murrow who led it.

In late 1953, Murrow was also joined by former president Harry Truman, who felt the need momentarily to leave the comfort of his home in Independence, Missouri, to go on radio and television and criticize the new Eisenhower administration for "embracing McCarthyism." Truman cut loose with a blistering attack not on Ike but on McCarthyism. He defined it as a "corruption of the truth, abandonment of our historical devotion to fair play, and of due process of law. It is the use of the Big Lie and the unfounded accusation against any citizen, in the name of Americanism and security. It is the rise to power of the demagogue who lives on untruth; it is the spread of fear and the destruction of faith at every level of our society."

One after another, very quickly, Murrow produced a series of *See It Now* programs aimed at the dangers McCarthy posed to the nation—at least as Murrow interpreted them. The series started with "An Argument in Indianapolis." The American Civil Liberties Union, the liberal ACLU, wanted to hold a meeting in the city, but the Indianapolis-based American Legion, pushing a conservative agenda, pressured one venue after another to say no, nothing was available. Finally, a Catholic priest offered his parish hall for the ACLU meeting. The American Legion had no trouble finding a convenient location for its own meeting. Murrow brought both meetings to the American people via split-screen TV.

Another program focused on Harry Dexter White, a former Treasury Department official in the Truman administration who was discovered to be slipping secrets to the Soviet Union. According to Ike's attorney general, Herbert Brownell, Truman appointed White to the job after being told that he was a Soviet spy, an allegation Truman vehemently denied. Still other programs dealt with sensitive issues, such as wiretaps, First Amendment rights, congressional hearings, and press freedom.

Finally, in February 1954, Murrow and Friendly both concluded, for a variety of reasons, that the time had come for the big broadcast. There were obvious risks—and opportunities—in being the first on television to confront McCarthy head-on. For one thing, McCarthy enjoyed high approval ratings—according to a Gallup poll, 46 percent of the American people still approved of him and his anticommunist witch hunt—even though he was getting into an embarrassing brouhaha with the White House and the U.S. Army, raising questions about his judgment and impetuousness. For another, McCarthy was capable of hurting CBS's bottom line and taunting Murrow as a "pinko" who had conspired with Moscow to infiltrate the American school system. But by proceeding with the program, Murrow could prove that television news had the guts to take on controversial issues and that he, personally and professionally, had the courage to oppose the rising tide of McCarthyism.

On Sunday, March 7, Murrow was in the CBS projection room, wearing his favorite flannel shirt and red suspenders. He wanted to pre-screen the assembled footage. All of his editors and reporters gathered around him. They watched the film. At this stage of production, it contained no narration. Murrow wondered whether they liked it. Interestingly, his film editors said yes, they did, but his reporters all thought it was rather flat, excessively neutral in tone. One thought that because it was based on McCarthy film clips, it would only serve to embolden his supporters. Murrow tended to agree. While powerful and informative, the film needed Murrow's commentary. He was ready to provide it.

An editor asked him what he was thinking of saying. "No one man can terrorize a whole nation," Murrow replied, "unless we are all his accomplices." He paused. "If none of us ever read a book that was 'dangerous,' had a friend who was 'different,' or joined an organization that advocated 'change,' we would all be just the kind of people Joe McCarthy wants." A reporter asked whether the White House might do "something" to stop McCarthy. Murrow snapped, "The White House is not going to do, and not going to say, one god-damned thing." He could just as well have said, it's up to us.

With Friendly at his side, Murrow asked every reporter and editor in the room whether there was anything in their lives, political or personal, that, if disclosed in the inevitable McCarthy backlash, might embarrass or hurt CBS, *See It Now*, or themselves. One editor said his divorced wife had been a communist before World War II. Many of the others shook their heads, or looked away. Murrow, his elbows on his knees, turned to Friendly. "The terror is right here in this room," he whispered, his brows knitted, a cigarette dangling from his lips. There was nothing cheerful in his voice or manner. "Ladies and gentlemen, thank you," he said, standing up. "We go with this Tuesday night."

Murrow spent all of Monday on his script. He wrote and rewrote every word. He filled his script with what he called "active words." When he arrived at Studio 41 in the Grand Central Terminal building on Tuesday evening for the pre-air rehearsal, he was beyond exhaustion but still focused, and very determined. In his hand was a script that would later appear in history books. At 10:30 p.m., the program opened on a grim-faced Murrow. He took the unusual step of reading directly from his script, no teleprompter. He wanted to be sure that he was saying exactly what he wrote. His subject, he began, was the danger of McCarthyism, nothing more or less, and, following Paley's advice, given to him earlier that day, he immediately offered McCarthy equal time, if the senator wanted it.

The program was essentially one film clip after another of McCarthy giving interviews, doing speeches, or interrogating witnesses with Murrow providing brief point-by-point rebuttals. For example:

- McCarthy waving what he described as "secret documents," Murrow saying the documents were publicly available for two dollars;

- McCarthy claiming the ACLU was a "communist front," Murrow showing it was supported by Truman, Eisenhower, and MacArthur;

- McCarthy protesting against "mud-slinging . . . by extreme left-wing elements of press and radio," Murrow reminding viewers of "freedom of the press" and reading portions of anti-McCarthy editorials that appeared in normally Republican newspapers;

- McCarthy asserting he would carry on his anticommunist crusade "regardless of who happens to be president" and quoting a line from Shakespeare, "Upon what meat does this our Caesar feed?," Murrow interjecting, "And upon what meat does Senator McCarthy feed? [His] investigations, protected by immunity, and the half-truth."

In a number of speeches, McCarthy was seen boasting about his successes but interrupting himself with odd, manic laughs that made him appear like a crazed fanatic. Murrow/Friendly made no effort to balance this image of McCarthy, for example with others showing him in a Santa outfit giving gifts to children at Christmas.

Never before on television had McCarthy's veracity been challenged, point by point. Never before on television had McCarthy been subjected to such a devastating indictment. And Murrow had not yet delivered his close, which was even more devastating. His voice, as always, was strong, his cadence measured, his manner very serious. "The line between investigating and persecuting is a very fine one," he began, "and the junior senator from Wisconsin has crossed over it repeatedly. . . . We must not confuse dissent with disloyalty. We must remember always that accusation is not proof and that conviction depends upon evidence and due process of law."

Murrow read his script as if it were gospel and kept looking up into camera, maintaining eye contact with his TV audience, measured in millions.

"We will not be driven by fear into an age of unreason," he continued, "if we dig deep into our own history and our doctrine and remember that we are not descended from fearful men, not from men who feared to write, to speak, to associate, and to defend causes which were for the moment unpopular. This is no time for men who oppose Senator McCarthy's methods to keep silent, or for those who approve. We can deny our heritage and our history, but we cannot escape responsibility for the result. There is no way for a citizen of a republic to abdicate his responsibilities.

"As a nation, we have come into our full inheritance at a tender age. We proclaim ourselves, as indeed we are, defenders of freedom—what's left of it—but we cannot defend freedom abroad by deserting it at home.

"The actions of the junior senator from Wisconsin have caused alarm and dismay amongst our allies abroad and given considerable aid and comfort to our enemies.

"And whose fault is that? Not really his; he didn't create this situation of fear, he merely exploited it and rather successfully."

For Murrow, World War II and the costs of unchecked Hitlerian aggression uppermost in his mind, his "responsibility" as a "citizen of a republic" was to speak up, and wake up the American people to the dangers of McCarthyism. The problem was—us. He concluded with a blunt verdict, again from Shakespeare. "Cassius was right," he said. "The fault, dear Brutus, is not in our stars but in ourselves. Good night and good luck."[2]

The immediate response to the program was overwhelmingly positive. Though there was some hostile comment (an organized postcard campaign accusing Murrow of "helping the forces that have weakened America"), most Americans loved the program and praised Murrow. When, the next day,

Murrow left CBS for the short walk to his club for lunch, he was of course recognized, and hundreds of people surrounded and cheered him, bringing traffic on Fifth Avenue to a complete stop. CBS reported the largest public response to a program it had ever measured—fifteen to one in Murrow's favor. Critic Jack Gould, writing in the *New York Times*, called the program "exciting, provocative, crusading journalism of high responsibility and genuine courage." This was "Mr. Murrow's and television's triumph, and a very great one." John Crosby of the *New York Herald Tribune* went, if possible, one step further. "Right there television came of age," he wrote, praising Murrow and CBS. "At least I can never recall any other time when a network—and Ed Murrow is a director as well as one of the chief spokesmen for CBS—has told its listeners to straighten up and act like free men with the clear implication that they are not now doing so." The *Herald Tribune* was a Republican newspaper. The *Times* and the *Herald Tribune* set the tone—similar praise appeared all over the country.

A few days later, Murrow attended the White House Correspondents' Association dinner in Washington. Though characteristically he played down his starring role in the program, his colleagues accorded him every honor to which he was surely entitled. Murrow was the star, and he was so treated. At one point during the cocktail hour, he felt a hand pressing playfully against his back. When he turned, he recognized a familiar grin. "Hello, Ed," chirped President Eisenhower, who had just made the effort to work his way through the crowds to greet Murrow. "I was just feeling to see if there were any knives sticking in it," a joking reference to any sharp criticism from McCarthy followers. Eisenhower, who had always feared McCarthy's political clout, was, in this gracious way, congratulating the reporter who had just shown the courage to take on the Wisconsin senator. Eisenhower and Murrow shook hands and laughed, as Murrow pointedly remarked, "From here on out, it's up to you, Mr. President." Up to this time, Republican politicians had given McCarthy a wide berth of political immunity, no matter how outrageous his conduct.

Columnists Joseph and Stewart Alsop, who witnessed the Eisenhower-Murrow handshake and later wrote about it, quipped, "No truer word was ever spoken. With McCarthy on the run," they judged, "the president has a golden opportunity to show once and for all who is the real leader of the Republican Party, and of the United States." The Alsops were thus disclosing what politicians and pundits were discussing in private—that, up until the Murrow program, McCarthy was seen by many as the unofficial leader of the Republican Party and of the country. But now Ike and his party had the chance to reclaim their legitimate authority, so downgraded did McCarthy seem after Murrow's blistering broadcast.

McCarthy himself attempted to take the high ground, an unusual vantage point for him. First he blasted the networks, especially CBS, as "dishonest," "arrogant," and "unmoral," and then had his wife tell inquiring reporters, with a straight face, that the senator had not seen the program because he had gone to bed early. "I never listen to the extreme left-wing, bleeding heart elements of radio and TV," he later explained. And yet he did accept an opportunity a few weeks later to reply to Murrow on television. The program aired on April 6, 1954. McCarthy accused Murrow of sponsoring, among other things, a "communist school in Moscow," which of course was unproven and nonsensical. With his broadcast, Murrow had placed McCarthy on a long, precarious slide to political oblivion. Even those who still tied their fortunes to the senator's crusade could see early signs of their hero's sudden vulnerabilities two days later, on

March 11, when his subcommittee heard testimony from Annie Lee Moss, an African American code clerk working for the U.S. Army. McCarthy, looking and acting oddly irrational, sounding as if he might have been drinking, dismissed Moss as "not of any great importance" herself, but added, "Who in the military, knowing that this lady was a Communist, promoted her from a waitress to a code clerk?" Army lawyers described her position as that of a "relay machine operator" handling "unintelligible" messages, and Moss gently but firmly denied that she was, or had ever been, a communist, had attended any meetings, paid any dues, or read the *Daily Worker*. She added that she didn't read any newspapers.

Annie Lee Moss seemed so unlikely a threat to the national security interests of the United States that McCarthy, though chair of the hearing, abruptly excused himself and left midway through her testimony. He claimed he had another appointment. TV cameras panned his empty seat, a symbol of his diminished political authority. The following Tuesday, Murrow did another broadcast on McCarthy's reckless attacks, this time against this aging, deeply religious widow, who happened to work as a code clerk for the U.S. Army. The Moss broadcast served as another nail in McCarthy's political coffin.

The Army-McCarthy Hearings

McCarthy had been investigating the Army Signal Corps for several months, claiming it had been "infested" with communists. An "espionage ring" existed, which had to be exposed, he said. Although he found nothing, he subjected General Ralph W. Zwicker, commanding officer of the Corps, to withering cross-examination. Violating all protocol, McCarthy called him "stupid" and accused him of having "the brains of a five-year-old child," adding he was "not fit to wear" his uniform. Many in the Pentagon were furious at the senator. Even Eisenhower was angry, urging the Army to fight back, which it finally did—but only after Murrow's program denouncing McCarthy. It released a report claiming McCarthy and his aide, Roy Cohn, had been pressuring the Army to give favored treatment to G. David Shine, a former McCarthy aide who had been drafted. Not true, McCarthy argued, counterclaiming that the Army was focusing on Shine only to discourage McCarthy from investigating the "espionage ring" in the Signal Corps.

The upshot of this claim and counterclaim was a Senate investigation that came to be called the Army-McCarthy hearings. They took place in the historic Senate Caucus Room, starting on April 22 and lasting until June 17. They were televised for 187 hours, and when it was all over, McCarthy was reduced further from a threat to a travesty. Some 22 million people, the estimated audience, watched some or all of the hearings. Many were repelled by McCarthy's antics, his frequent, snarling interruptions, his obviously unfair harassing of witnesses, and his repeated calls for "a point of order," which turned him into a joke on radio and television.

The climactic moment came on June 9, when McCarthy suddenly attacked a young lawyer from the Boston law firm of Joseph Welch, who represented the Army in these hearings. Welch, fed up with McCarthy's constant badgering and insults, leaned over and tearfully observed, "Until this moment, Senator, I think I never really gauged your cruelty, or your recklessness. Let us not assassinate this lad further, Senator. You have done enough." He spoke in a soft voice, making it all the more compelling. "Have you no sense of decency, sir,

at long last? Have you left no sense of decency?" The questions would make their way into history books. "If it were in
my power to forgive you for your reckless cruelty," Welch concluded, suggesting only God had such power, "I would do so.
I like to think I'm a gentle man, but your forgiveness will have
to come from someone other than me." McCarthy attempted
at this point to intervene, but Welch cut him off and called
another witness. The Army-McCarthy hearings ended incon-
clusively a few days later.

The End of McCarthyism

Politicians often judge reality by poll numbers, and, after Murrow's broadcast on McCarthy, the numbers sang a new song.
As late as March 2, a week before Murrow's historic broadcast, McCarthy still enjoyed a 46 percent approval rating.
Although many Republican politicians, most especially one
named Eisenhower, disliked, distrusted, and disagreed with
McCarthy, they still did not feel they could act against him—
he was simply too popular with rank-and-file party members.
But after the Murrow broadcast, Gallup produced polls that
put a spine in a number of GOP backs—or at least a modest
degree of courage to take a first step against the once invincible
senator from Wisconsin. On March 24, before the Army-
McCarthy hearings even got started, McCarthy's approval
rating had already dropped to 32 percent, where it remained
throughout the hearings. The 14 percent drop, attributed to the
enthusiastic public response to the Murrow broadcast, encouraged three Republican senators to begin the delicate process of
censuring a colleague. They were Ralph Flanders of Vermont,
Arthur Watkins of Utah, and the senator who had first spoken

up against McCarthy four years earlier, Margaret Chase Smith of Maine.

On June 11 Flanders offered a resolution to strip McCarthy of his committee and subcommittee chairmanships, but few of his colleagues wanted to tinker with the seniority system, which effectively chose committee chairs. Even so, McCarthy began losing stature within his committees.

On August 2 the Senate cautiously decided that rather than investigate McCarthy's anticommunist crusade, which was the heart of McCarthyism, it would focus on his violations of Senate procedures, of which there were many. Following an old custom, the Senate set up a bipartisan select committee, consisting of three Republicans and three Democrats, notable for their impeccable reputations and legal expertise, and requested a report by the end of business for the Eighty-third Congress. Watkins, selected as chair of the committee, plotted each move with exquisite care. After weeks of secret hearings, the committee found itself burdened with forty-six counts of misconduct, which it arbitrarily cut to five, to make the process more manageable. On September 27, it produced a public report that cut the five counts to two: McCarthy's refusal to appear before earlier committees looking into his gross misconduct, and his public abuse and defamation of General Zwicker.

On November 8, after the midterm election, the Senate convened in a rare lame-duck session to reach a verdict on McCarthy. In the ensuing debate, McCarthy labeled the select committee the "unwitting handmaiden of the Communist Party," attacked Watkins as "cowardly," and called the entire proceeding a "lynch party." Watkins responded with a passionate plea for Senate dignity, which prompted a round of cheers from the galleries.

On December 2, the Senate voted 67-22 to censure McCarthy "for his non-cooperation with and abuse of the Subcommittee on Privileges and Elections in 1952" and "for abuse of the Select Committee to Study Censure" in 1954. The Senate took no stand on his hunt-for-communists crusade and its ugly effect on American politics and society, censuring him only for his repeated violations of Senate behavioral norms.

With McCarthy suddenly on the ropes, Murrow had more than a few moments to contemplate the impact of his March 9 broadcast, and he found himself returning again and again to the incredible power of television and, as important, to the failure of the networks to act sooner, creating "a great conspiracy of silence."

In the wrong hands, or directed toward an immoral end, television could "some day be employed to damage or dishonor free government," Murrow warned. "Is it not possible," he asked, "that an infectious smile, eyes that seem remarkable for the depths of their sincerity, a cultivated air of authority, may attract a huge television audience, regardless of the violence that may be done to truth and objectivity?" Murrow was fully persuaded that his March 9 broadcast had to be done, but, long after, he continued to worry about the power of television in the wrong hands. He had to stop McCarthy, but he often brushed aside the compliments he received for doing the program.

"It's a sad state of affairs," he said, reflecting years later on the McCarthy adventure, "when people think I'm courageous to do this. . . . The timing was right and the instrument powerful. We did it fairly well, with a degree of restraint and credibility. There was a great conspiracy of silence at that time. When there is such a conspiracy and somebody makes a loud noise, it attracts all the attention."

True, but Murrow did it, when no one else could—or would.

NINE

"Otherwise, It Is Not America"

IF, WHEN MURROW LIVED IN ENGLAND, an Oxford don had approached him and asked for a definition of "America," he would likely have given him the same definition he gave me many years later. America was, of course, a country, but Murrow also thought of it as an idea—and the idea was that precious gift called freedom. How would he have defined "freedom"? In two ways. "The only thing that counts is the right to know, to speak, to think," Murrow once told a friend, "that!—and the sanctity of the courts. Otherwise, it is not America." The man from a log cabin in North Carolina defined his country in the language of constitutional legitimacy: a place, where people could be assured of their First Amendment rights, including freedom of the press, and where the "sanctity of the courts" was an accepted principle of governance: everyone entitled to a fair trial and no one considered above the law. "Otherwise," as Murrow said, "it is not America."

Donald Trump's vision of "America" would have collided with Murrow's, and it would have alarmed him—first, because of Trump's ugly running war with the press, and second, because of his continuing attacks on the judicial system. For Murrow, "freedom of the press" and "sanctity of the courts" were basic to American democracy, and Trump was trampling on both.

The Trump Challenge

From the beginning of his presidency, which Trump regarded as just another branch of his sprawling business empire, Trump seemed to have forgotten that he swore his allegiance to the U.S. Constitution, assuming for a moment that he had ever read and understood the underlying principles of this foundational document. By his words and actions, he seems to have displayed less an allegiance to democracy than to a form of personal authoritarianism, suggesting he places his personal and family needs (and whims) above his respect for the law.

Trump has rejected the traditional view that the Justice Department should operate independently of the White House. In Trump's view, the Justice Department exists to protect him. Trump speaks of Attorney General Jeff Sessions as if he were his personal attorney and not the head of the nation's top law enforcement agency, and he speaks of the Federal Bureau of Investigation (FBI) as if it were a secret gang of gun-toting mercenaries bent on undercutting his presidency.

The upshot is that Trump has opened an unprecedented war against both, calling the Justice Department "really, really disgraceful" and saying the FBI "should be ashamed," the "worst in history," its reputation "in tatters." No other chief executive has ever sought to demolish the reputation of the Justice Department. And for what purpose? Trump hoped to damage and, if possible, destroy Special Counsel Robert S. Mueller III's investigation of alleged collusion in 2016 between the Trump campaign and Vladimir Putin's Russia.

"I can't think of another time when this has happened," said Harvard law professor Jack L. Goldsmith, who held a senior position in President George W. Bush's Justice Department. "And it's happening largely because the president is being investigated."

Trump's relentless assault on the FBI has had a major impact on public opinion, and it's been helpful to the president. The GOP used to be among the FBI's strongest supporters, with overwhelming majorities backing even its most reckless intrusions into the personal lives of private citizens. Now, according to recent surveys, only 38 percent of Republicans have a favorable opinion of the FBI, and the figure continues to drop. By comparison, 64 percent of Democrats have a positive view of the FBI. Trump wanted to hurt the reputation of the FBI solely because he perceives it as a threat to him, and in this respect he has succeeded. Now, assuming for a moment that Trump was charged with collusion with Russia, he could, and probably would, dismiss it as "fake news," part of a "witch hunt," knowing all the while that his base would agree with him, not with the special counsel.

Perhaps even more troubling is Trump's assault on the judiciary—one of three coequal branches of the U.S. government, according to the Constitution. Trump's belittling and demeaning of judges who cross him is unprecedented. When District Judge Gonzalo Curiel ruled against Trump in a case involving certain questionable practices at Trump University,

Trump attacked not only the judge's ruling but also his Mexican heritage. When District Judge William H. Orrick ruled against his travel ban on Muslims from nations where terrorism thrives, Trump called it an "egregious order by a single, unelected judge." When a judge ruled against his decision to restrict federal funding for sanctuary cities, Trump ripped into the entire judicial system, warning that the "so-called judges," as he put it, not he, would be held responsible for any terrorist attack in the United States.

Such a sustained attack on the entire judicial system is extremely dangerous. Every other president seems to have understood the need for an independent judiciary, all except Trump, who regards the judiciary as an annoying impediment to his style of personalized governance.

Burke, Carlyle, Murrow—and Trump?

For a president who has discarded his daily written intelligence briefing because he thinks he gets more out of a short oral briefing and because, in any case, he sees little purpose to it, the thought that he might spend some time reading Edmund Burke or Thomas Carlyle for insights into better government is, granted, far-fetched. But if he did read these exceptional British philosophers, he might learn something about the importance of the press in a democracy, assuming he could think of the press as more than just a tool for his own ego satisfaction.

Shortly after the publication of his classic history of the French Revolution, Carlyle reflected on one of Burke's many valuable observations about democratic rule. "There were three estates in Parliament," Burke noted, linking the British system of government with the American system, "but, in the Reporters' Gallery yonder, there sat a Fourth Estate more important far than they all." From this observation, more than any other, arose the concept of the press as a fourth branch of government, and it has held through history, gaining power and obliging Carlyle to observe, "A Fourth Estate, of Able Editors, springs up, increases and multiplies; irrepressible, incalculable." Both writers made clear that the fourth estate would likely be rambunctious, opinionated, expansive in influence and scope—and most certainly not part of the government. The other three estates (or branches, in modern parlance) composed the government; only the fourth estate stood outside of it, proud possessor of a unique responsibility: to observe and report on the other three estates "without fear or favor," to quote a *New York Times* publisher. The independence of the fourth estate was, and remains, a special feature of American democracy.

Murrow was a fan of both Burke and Carlyle and believed deeply that a free press ensures a free society and deserves a special place of honor in any democracy. It should be praised, not scorned or insulted, and never should it be thought of as an "enemy of the people." Quite the contrary. The press spreads facts and opinions, holds governments to account, serves as a loop for getting information from the public back to the government, sparks endless discussions about the rights and wrongs of society, and ensures the survival and strength of democratic rule. Hence, when a threat arises against a free press, it is a problem not just for journalists but for every citizen who wants information free from government control. Trump's nonstop attacks on the press—on the "failing *New York Times*," for example, or on reporters as "the most dishonest people in the world"—constitute a direct challenge to American democracy, the most serious challenge a president has ever hurled at the press.

Attacking Both the Judiciary and the Press

On February 17, 2017, inspired, as we now know, by the disgruntled Democratic pollster Pat Caddell, Trump ramped up his running war with the media, mindlessly resurrecting one of the ugliest phrases of the twentieth century and directing it at the American press: "enemy of the American people," he blathered. He used it a few more times early in his administration (it sparked a powerfully negative response, especially from reporters), and he chose to rely more frequently on the less inflammatory but more effective phrase, "fake news," and it worked. A few weeks before his election in 2016, Trump had boasted to TV host and former governor Mike Huckabee, "One of the greatest of all terms I've come up with is 'fake.'" Again, he did not know the historical roots of "fake news," which had been around for a long time, but he stumbled upon it during his campaign, and when he found it to be a useful political tool, he employed it repeatedly as president. It became his standout slur and *Collins Dictionary*'s "Word of the Year" for 2017.

His intent in blasting the press was no different from his deliberate demeaning of the judiciary—to downgrade and diminish the independent role of both in a democracy, and in this way to pump up his ego, to rally his base, and to protect his position as "master of the universe."

At of mid-2018, judging by public opinion polls, Trump has emerged as the winner of his war with the press, in part because the press is an easy target for demagogues—it operates in public, warts and all on full display—but also because the press remains more intent on covering the president than in fighting him. Although Frank Newport, Gallup's editor in chief, reports with a sigh of relief that a majority of Americans still consider the media to be "critical or important to democracy," he still notes that a healthy and growing minority, 43 percent, hold a decidedly negative view of the press. Polling by the Poynter Institute, released in December 2017, tends to parallel Gallup's numbers, but ends up painting a more negative picture.[1]

- One out of three Americans, says Poynter, believes the press is, as Trump charged, the "enemy of the American people."

- 31 percent say the media is "preventing" political leaders from doing their job.

- 67 percent accept Trump's view of sexual harassment claims against him, saying it's all "fake news."

- 25 percent feel the government should have the right to stop publication of stories it considers "biased or inaccurate," which would be a direct violation of the First Amendment guarantee of "freedom of the press."

- An *Axios*/SurveyMonkey poll, conducted June 15–19, 2018, said "nearly all Republicans and Republican-leaning independents (92%) think that traditional news outlets knowingly report false or misleading stories, at least sometimes." Fifty-three percent of Democrats or Democrat-leaning independents were said to believe the same thing about the press. But where can the serious citizen get trustworthy news, if not from the press? The press is the essential middleman for information. If the press is not trusted, then the government can say whatever it wants—and get away with it.[2]

- In a *Politico*-Morning Consult poll, 74 percent of Democrats said they "trust" the media; only 19 percent of Republicans did. This is a perfect mirror image of the deep divide in American politics, which has existed for several administrations. Again, Trump is not the sole reason for the great divide, but he has exploited it—and made it much worse.[3]

So far, all polls in the Trump era seem to reflect the president's remarkable ability to read, influence, and change public opinion, especially among Republicans. One example: during and even after the Cold War, Republicans have been reliably anti-Russian and anticommunist. Now, because Trump has thrown himself into a strange love affair with Vladimir Putin and the Russians, much of the GOP has switched its position on Russia. No explanation has been offered, but now many Republicans have begun to sound like Democrats, and Democrats like the Republicans of old, with the GOP apparently hoping for some sort of big Trump/Putin deal, and the Democrats not believing either president can really deliver or be trusted.

To drive home his point, whether about Russia or taxes, Trump follows the example of a number of twentieth-century dictators who repeated their lies so often people thought the lies were truths. A White House source told *Axios*'s Mike Allen, "He just hammers something into submission, whatever it may be. . . . With the media, he just wears it down, wears it down," until, Allen added, a reporter makes a mistake covering Trump, and the president leaps on the mistake and uses it as proof that none of the media can be trusted. Most Republicans believe and trust the president, not the media (except for Fox News, of course), and an alarming number have begun to wonder why America still needs freedom of the press, a right guaranteed by the First Amendment.

In 1945, the astute British writer, George Orwell, author of the dark political satire *Nineteen Eighty-Four,* wrote, "If large numbers of people believe in freedom of speech, there will be freedom of speech, even if the law forbids it. But if public opinion is sluggish, inconvenient minorities will be prosecuted, even if laws exist to protect them." So much, in his view, depended on public opinion, more important on occasion than even the law.

Trump's persistent devaluing of the press as "fake news" has caused considerable damage to the concept of freedom of the press and therefore to one of democracy's most basic principles. For example, in July 2017, NBC News reported that the president was planning a major expansion of the American nuclear arsenal, a fact the president immediately labeled "fake news," even though he knew it was true. Trump tweeted that the report was "pure fiction made up to demean" him, and, in anger, he threatened to strip NBC of its broadcasting license. Trump obviously did not know that he, even as president, had no such power—the FCC licenses individual stations, not networks. Still, he sounded tough, a network was threatened, and his conservative base, which distrusts the media in any case, was delighted.

Trump Dominates the News Cycle

Covering Trump in the era of twenty-four-hour news cycles can be an exhausting business. Networks and newspapers have assigned additional reporters to the White House, and that's costly. For example, pre-Trump, the *New York Times* had two reporters covering the White House; now it has six. Mike Allen of *Axios* on December 1, 2017, outlined an average day in the life of Trump coverage.[4]

Sometime between 6 and 7 a.m., timed to help *Fox and Friends* on Fox cable news, his favorite program on his favorite network, Trump lights up Twitter with a news bombshell, whatever the subject. Within minutes, his message is retweeted by hundreds of thousands of his followers (an estimated 51 million now receive his message on a regular basis), and then re-retweeted before 9 a.m. by critical viewers of *Morning Joe* on MSNBC and by political activists ready to pounce, pro or con, on the president's latest tweet.

At 9 a.m., the cable world, which drives much of the day's news, snaps into action, as CNN, Fox, and MSNBC try to match and outmatch one another, bursting at the seams with what they often mistakenly hype as "breaking news."

From 9 a.m. to 6 p.m., it's a nonstop struggle as reporters and commentators, loaded with opinions and news, join their cable hosts for an endless critique of the president's early morning tweet or tweets. "They tweet the highlights," *Axios* explains. "The rage builds. The cycle speeds." The fringe players enter the fray at different times in the day. *Breitbart*, Rush Limbaugh, and the *Drudge Report* occupy one corner of the ring, fighting on the president's side. CNN, led by Wolf Blitzer and Jake Tapper, occupies another corner, trying to sound neutral. The websites of the mainstream media engage all corners in a never-ending struggle to be first with a break-ing story.

Finally, though the sun sets, the battle only intensifies. MSNBC enters the fray dramatically from the left, attack-ing the White House and Trump. Fox enters just as dramati-cally from the right, undercutting the Democrats, attacking all Trump critics, and praising the president. It's the nightly battle of cable gladiators, Maddow vs. Hannity, fifteen rounds before a full house. By midnight, the stars go to bed, and the wan-nabees try through the night to persuade the dwindling but committed band of warrior-viewers to believe that their cable networks are still "breaking news."

And at 6 a.m. the next day, the battle resumes all over again.

Enter the Internet and the New Revolution

The internet, like the Gutenberg Bible in the 1400s, has touched off a revolution in the way we communicate with one another. We are lurching from print to the web at a startling speed, and, within ten years, there may no longer be a print edition even of the *New York Times*. CEO Mark Thompson has bluntly stated that the "economics no longer make sense for us." Of course, he wants the *Times* to "survive and thrive as long as it can," but, putting the best face on the wild web ride, he could not count on more than "ten years" for "our print products" to hold on in the United States.

Not just the *Times* but all newspapers, large and small, have been severely challenged by the rise of the internet. Commer-cial ads, on which the newspapers depended for their operating budgets, have fled to television or the web, leaving the entire newspaper universe in a state described by one senior editor as "fragile." Even covering middle America has become problematic, but covering the rest of the world has become especially problematic. As budgets have been cut, so too have foreign bureaus—and the space for foreign news has shrunk, even for newspapers such as the *Times*. It could be argued that the world has become so mercurial, so unpredictable and dangerous, that now more than ever, it cries out for more thoughtful, wide-ranging coverage. But with budgets tight, and with coverage so heavily focused on a Trump presidency that demands twenty-four-hour-a-day reporting, there may not be enough funding for foreign coverage, denying readers the opportunity to learn about the rest of the world, which also operates on a twenty-four-hour-a-day schedule. We may soon be reaching a point in American journalism where foreign news is reserved in local newspapers for half a column on an inside page, a minute or two of television time on the local news, or a few lonely websites reserved for foreign policy specialists, nothing more. Major newspapers, such as the *New York Times*, may still cover the world, but often need financial help, or they would not be able to.

Again, Trump did not create this problem; he only exacerbated and exploited it.

Enter an organization, such as the Pulitzer Center on Crisis Reporting,* which, in addition to teaching about the value and importance of a free press, provides funding to journalists—and news outlets—to help cover the world. One example out of many: in August 2016, the *New York Times Magazine* was able to devote an entire issue to a report on the Middle East

---

*I have been senior adviser to the Pulitzer Center for the past five years.

titled "Fractured Lands," written by Scott Anderson and photographed by Paolo Pellegrin. It was able to do this remarkable report because the Pulitzer Center contributed $150,000 to the two reporters and to the *Times Magazine*. Otherwise it would not have been done, and readers would have lost this chance to learn about an explosive part of the world that could, without warning, force the United States into another war. For an additional $50,000, Anderson was then able to travel to dozens of American colleges and universities as well as secondary schools to tell students about his reporting from the Middle East. It was the Pulitzer Center's way of lighting fires under a new generation of students—to encourage them to learn about journalism and to care about people and places all over the world.

The Pulitzer Center and only a few other such institutions now fill this urgent need for supplemental funding to cover world events, their way of alerting Americans to a world beyond Trumpian scandals and Washington investigations. The president sucks up too much of Washington's precious supply of oxygen, leaving news organizations little option but to cover one Trump-related story after another, ignoring or downplaying much of the rest of the nation and the world. The work of the Pulitzer Center is one way of filling the holes, while all of journalism—print, broadcast, and web—struggles to find the right financial formula for covering local, national, and global news.

From Murrow to Cronkite to Woodward and Bernstein

In the context of the press's struggle to cover the world of Trump and beyond, it's important to recall that Murrow, in his memorable 1954 *See It Now* broadcast about Senator McCarthy, helped bring an end to a political crusade that was frightening the American people and undermining American democracy. He exposed McCarthy as a lying charlatan who deserved the Senate censure he was to suffer a few months later. Though many other reporters covered the same story, only Murrow will likely be remembered as the one who had the courage to take on a senator widely considered to be a danger to the republic. In American history, few other reporters have played so prominent a role in ending a national nightmare.

Cronkite, Stalemate, and the Vietnam War

Walter Cronkite, another of CBS's twinkling stars, whose even-handed anchoring of the CBS Evening News won him the title "the most trusted man in America," did a commentary about the Vietnam War in February 1968 that helped persuade a president not to run for reelection and a nation to change its war policy and, ultimately, begin to withdraw.

A month earlier, the North Vietnamese had launched their consequential Tet Offensive. From one end of South Vietnam to the other, they attacked South Vietnamese and American troops and bases, even invading the once-hallowed grounds of the U.S. embassy in Saigon. To say President Lyndon Johnson was stunned by the news would be a glaring understatement. His intelligence chiefs had assured him that the communists were losing the war. General William Westmoreland, U.S. commanding general in Vietnam, had told Congress a few months earlier that he saw "the light at the end of the tunnel." When, after Tet, Westmoreland approached Johnson with a request for an additional 206,000 troops, Johnson, who had always said yes to his commanding general, now snapped "no," not only to the request but to his own plans for reelection. The war proved to be too much, even for this rugged Texan, and he decided on the spot to end all political games—he would not run! Behind his fateful decision was the amazing story of a Cronkite commentary and the impact it had on a president.

It could be said that Cronkite was "disillusioned" with the war from the very beginning. "Disillusioned" was the word he used in his memoir, published years later. But, on air, when he anchored the top-rated CBS Evening News, he was always meticulously fair, the impartial newscaster, never an editorial grimace or nod of approval, never a word suggesting an opinion. Eric Sevareid did the commentary. "Uncle Walter" did the news. "And that's the way it is," was Cronkite's closing signature every evening. That was what many viewers had come to expect.

With the Tet Offensive still hot news, splashed all over the front pages, Cronkite asked CBS president Richard Salant if he could go to Vietnam and do an "assessment" of the war as someone who had not "previously taken a public position." Salant nodded, and Cronkite left that night. This was not his first war; Cronkite had covered World War II. In Vietnam, after talking to American and South Vietnamese generals and to the troops, he found he could reach only one conclusion: "There was no way that this war could be justified any longer," he said.

After a few days, Cronkite flew back to New York, where he anchored a special report, aired on February 27, 1968, about the effect of the Tet Offensive on the war. He was gloomy, clearly disturbed by what he had seen, and he closed his report with a commentary, so labeled. Only twice before had he done a commentary, and the anchorman justified both by saying they focused on a defense of a free press. This one was different. This was Cronkite giving his personal opinion about one of the most controversial issues of the day—the war in Vietnam. Salant warned America's "most trusted man" that he could be jeopardizing his reputation, CBS's as well, and, given the public's sharply divided opinion about the war, he could also be risking the loss of many viewers, thereby hurting CBS's bottom line. (Murrow had considered the same possibilities when he did his McCarthy broadcast fourteen years earlier.) Cronkite listened carefully to Salant but decided he had to go forward and express his opinion about the war. It was his journalistic obligation, he felt.

Cronkite explained on air that he was doing a "commentary" on the war. He wrote it himself. "To say that we are closer to victory today," he said solemnly, "is to believe, in the face of the evidence, the optimists who have been wrong in the past. To suggest we are on the edge of defeat is to yield to unreasonable pessimism. To say that we are mired in stalemate seems the only realistic, yet unsatisfactory, conclusion." Cronkite paused, looked into the camera lens, and, in an uncharacteristically soft voice, concluded, "It is increasingly clear to this reporter that the only rational way out, then, will be to negotiate, not as victors, but as an honorable people who lived up to their pledge to defend democracy, and did the best they could." Cronkite clearly implied that if a stalemate was the "best" we could hope for, after having lost so many troops, spent so much money, and torn the country apart, then it took no special insight to believe that the United States could not possibly win this war, and therefore we ought to pull out of it.

The public reaction to Cronkite's extraordinary broadcast was amazingly unenthusiastic. Those who supported Johnson and the war were critical of Cronkite, but not overly so. Those who opposed the war applauded Cronkite, but again not overly so. It seemed as if the public was simply tired of the war, and Cronkite's commentary did not move the needle decisively one way or the other. He didn't call for an immediate withdrawal of American forces or for a dramatic escalation of the war. His instincts as a network anchor kept him close to the middle rail—a call to negotiate in the face of a stalemate. In this respect, even someone as revered as Cronkite probably came through as just another voice in the crowd.

But, at the White House, Cronkite's voice, always special, carried a powerful message. Johnson listened intently; what he heard stunned him. George Christian, his news secretary, and Bill Moyers, his personal assistant, were present when a shaken Johnson watched the program. "The President flipped off the set," Moyers later recalled, "and said, 'If I've lost Cronkite, I've lost middle America.'" Five weeks later, Johnson went on television in prime time to announce that he would not run for reelection and would begin to negotiate an end to the war—if possible on America's terms. But Hanoi had other plans.

Journalist David Halberstam, thinking about the impact of Cronkite's commentary, later wrote that it was probably the first time in history that a network anchor declared a war to be over. But the war would not be over until 1975. Johnson did not live to see the end. He died in 1973.

Woodward and Bernstein—and Watergate

On June 17, 1972, a team of burglars was arrested for breaking into the headquarters of the Democratic National Committee at the Watergate complex in Washington. Two young reporters at the *Washington Post*, Bob Woodward and Carl Bernstein, soon began covering the story that led, in August 1974, to the first resignation of an American president and to profound changes in the nation's politics. Would Richard Nixon have resigned anyway, even if Woodward and Bernstein had not applied their considerable investigative skills to breaking the Watergate story? I doubt it. Their remarkable run of one exclusive story after another kept a steady spotlight on the puzzling break-in: Who were the burglars? Who paid them? Why the Democratic headquarters? Was the Nixon White House involved? What was Nixon's role? These questions framed the Watergate scandal, which will always be associated with the reporting of Woodward and Bernstein.

Within a matter of weeks, the reporters learned that the grand jury investigating the break-in had sought testimony from two men who had worked in the White House—former CIA officer E. Howard Hunt and former FBI agent G. Gordon Liddy—thus linking the break-in to the White House. Soon Bernstein discovered in Miami that a $25,000 check for Nixon's reelection had been deposited in the bank account of one of the burglars, suggesting the White House paid the burglar. How else would he have obtained the check? A White House lawyer, John Dean, observing the illegal shenanigans around him, privately told Nixon that, in his judgment, there was "a cancer on the presidency." At first Nixon did not believe him. When he finally did believe Dean, it was too late to save his presidency.

Watergate had quickly become a hot story, and, with Woodward and Bernstein, the *Post* had struck gold. Their diligent, carefully researched stories, leading to journalistic prizes and a Hollywood movie, touched off a series of investigations involving Congress, special prosecutors, federal judges, the FBI, and the CIA that, by the summer of 1974, led to the inescapable conclusion that the president had lied in attempting to obstruct justice, and, if he wanted to escape impeachment, he would be wise to resign, which is what Nixon did on August 9, 1974.

The possibility must be acknowledged that the Nixon administration might have been toppled even without the reporting of Woodward and Bernstein. Too many loose ends were being investigated. Too many insiders were talking. Perhaps more important, the Democrats controlled Congress, and they did not like Nixon. Other news organizations, including the *New York Times* and CBS, were also digging into the Watergate scandal and producing their own exclusives. "What did the president know and when did he know it?" was a question for discussion on Capitol Hill and across the country. Everyone was into Watergate. Everyone had an opinion. Well before Nixon announced his resignation, his days seemed to be numbered.

Woodward and Bernstein deserve their pages in the history of American journalism. Their reporting contributed to the unraveling of the Watergate scandal, but, for the sake of argument, what if there had been a Fox News channel in the early 1970s? Dan Shelley, executive director of the Radio Television Digital News Association, has wondered whether Nixon, protected by a chattering conservative cable news channel, might have survived the scandal. Every evening, a Sean Hannity would have been arguing the president's case.

A Laura Ingraham would have been challenging the *Post*'s patriotism and criticizing Woodward and Bernstein as "liberal puppets of the anti-Nixon Democratic cabal." GOP senators would have had a soapbox of their own to question press and TV coverage of Nixon. Fox would happily have joined with *Breitbart* and Limbaugh to create a dark Wagnerian opera of right-wing commentary that likely would have changed the political conversation and softened the impact of front-page Woodward-and-Bernstein stories. The embattled president would have enjoyed a measure of support from conservative media that in 1974 he surely did not have. And the result of the Watergate scandal might have been different. We'll never know.

Trump Capitalizes on Media Revolution

What we do know is that much has changed in American journalism and politics since Murrow's anti-McCarthy broadcast in 1954 (that's sixty-four years ago), Cronkite's broadcast in 1968 (fifty years ago), and Woodward and Bernstein's reporting of the Watergate scandal from 1972 to 1974. In the intervening years, we have experienced at least two major revolutions that have transformed the practice of journalism—one on the business side and the other in technology.

Since the 1980s, local newspapers and radio and TV stations, once owned by local businessmen and their families, have been snapped up by national media corporations far more interested in short-term profits than in public service. In the past, broadcast news was not expected to make much money, and it rarely did. Today's economics, however, requires profitability, and this fundamentally changes the dynamics of the news business. Now it must make money or be discarded as a rusty wreck. Ratings (and profits or losses) now dominate conversation in and about the news business. CNN popped onto the scene in the early 1980s, disparaged in those days as the Chicken Noodle Network. It didn't make money then; it does now—an estimated $1 billion in 2016. Fox and MSNBC joined the cable hit parade in the mid-1990s. Within ten years, they too began to make money; within twenty years, lots of money. Since Trump arrived on the political scene, they've made tons of money. He has been their meal ticket—they knew it, and he knew it. Money, not quality, became the measure of journalistic success. Even journalists who knew better bent to the pressure. They had no choice.

The other revolution, in technology, changed everything, so much so that now the broadcast networks have yielded to cable for most political news and commentary, especially in the evening, and newspapers have had to face the real prospect of soon terminating their print editions and then surviving, if possible, as websites in the new and highly competitive internet worlds of web and social media. Who would have imagined, even a few years ago, that a president would discuss vital issues of war and peace on his Twitter account? A president who would watch cable news four to eight hours a day? A president who would see a day at the White House as a reality TV show? A president who would turn a State of the Union address into a television show? Or a president who would attack the press as an "enemy of the American people"?

Not Murrow, nor Cronkite, nor Woodward and Bernstein could possibly be re-created to cover the political wars of the Trump era. In one lifetime we have lived through lightning changes in standards and morality, affecting our journalism and our politics; and if we are all left a bit bewildered, that can be excused. In many respects, I add most reluctantly, journalism has become a form of entertainment, especially on television. Murrow could not survive today—probably not Cronkite either. There are many investigative reporters, maybe not as good as Woodward and Bernstein, but very accomplished nonetheless. Those who work for the *New York Times* and the *Washington Post* now perform the role Murrow played in the early 1950s. Other news organizations, such as *Politico*, McClatchy, MSNBC, CNN, and occasionally the *Wall Street Journal*, also come up with their exclusives, but they often follow the two print leaders. Murrow took on McCarthy, and won the day. Now, the *Times* and the *Post* take on Trump, though their editors deny that is what they are doing. "Just covering the news," they say. In any case, the battle for truth is far from won, partly because journalism as an ongoing enterprise is so fragile (and yet so essential to American democracy) and partly because the story focuses on the most important yet most erratic politician in the country and perhaps the world.

Moreover, adding complexity to the coverage is the eruption of social media websites that convey, among other things, information as "news" or something vaguely resembling news—sites such as Facebook, Google, YouTube, Twitter, and the like. These sites do not provide all of the news people need and use, but more people now depend on these sites for their news than on more traditional mainstream sources, such as local TV, national newspapers, and cable and broadcast news networks. It is unclear whether people who depend for their news on, say, Facebook are as well read and informed as those who depend on the *Times* and the *Post*, but, for the people who set the national agenda, whether politicians or journalists, the *Times* or the *Post*—or both—still are must reading. It is a safe bet that both the strategist who sits on the National Security Council and the editor of *BuzzFeed* or even *Breitbart* starts his or her day by reading the *Times*, the *Post*, or both.

TEN

A Free Press, Now More Than Ever

WITH TRUMP, WITTINGLY OR not, stumbling toward a form of political authoritarianism, the press, imperfect though it be, must continue to play a central role, covering him boldly and bravely. There is no other option.

American politics and governance have entered uncharted waters. On any given day, we seem to be on the edge of another 1973 Saturday Night Massacre, or worse. Nightmarish visions of a president at war with the judiciary and of streets filled with angry mobs and perhaps even armed troops crowd the corners of the public's imagination and fill many hearts with fear.

What might, in fact, emerge from the political madness that now defines Trump's Washington? Consider these scenarios:

Could we, if we had a chance to look back, realistically have expected the Republican-led Senate or House to convene an emergency investigation of the Trump campaign's collusion with Russia, when the Republicans on the House Intelligence Committee have already insisted there was no collusion? Could we have expected the House Judiciary Committee to begin impeachment hearings of President Trump? Could we have expected Vice President Mike Pence, acting under the Twenty-fifth Amendment, to form a special committee of key cabinet officials to ponder the imponderable—Trump's removal from office because, they would argue, he was "unfit" to serve? And what in the final analysis could we have expected of this beleaguered president, who had always claimed there was "no collusion" between his campaign and the Russians? Would he have quietly accepted the results of a special counsel's investigation, whatever they might be? Or would he, more characteristically, have doubled down and fought, exploiting the street-corner anger of his political supporters?

In this darkening miasma, so much truly depends on the man in the middle of the storm. Would it be too late to imagine a sudden burst of political normalcy from the White House, a return to a time when America's chief executive respected the judiciary and honored the role of the press in our democracy? If Trump could refer to himself as a "very stable genius," then the problem we face appears to be more than one of definition. He is delusional. But Trump, being Trump, enjoys the tumult and confusion. He is the center of attention, the lead story in the newspaper, the lead item on the evening news. And that is when he is happiest, most himself—a man who looks at the world through a mirror.

Trump's "Well-Documented Disregard for Truth"

If you were to compare the Trump administration with the Nixon, Reagan, and Clinton administrations, you would find that Trump has learned nothing from history. He appears, in the words of *Washington Post* book critic Carlos Lozada, "Nixonian in his disregard for democratic norms, Clintonian in his personal recklessness and beyond Reaganesque in his distance from the details of policy." No comparison works, however, when considering his "well-documented disregard for truth." Trump gives every reason to believe that he is truly a congenital liar. Nothing from his lips can any longer be accepted as truthful. He conveys the clear impression of a conniving huckster, for whom, Lozada wrote, "the expectation of integrity has given way to a cynical acceptance of deceit." For Trump, deceit has become the norm, leaving not only the nation but the world in a state of confusion and anxiety. He lies as often, it seems, as he violates diplomatic protocol.[1]

It is hard to believe, but in his first year in office he never once hosted a state dinner for a foreign leader—not the prime minister of the United Kingdom, an obvious candidate, nor the chancellor of Germany, a reliable ally. He had, in fact, dismissive words for both, saving his compliments for such autocrats as Russia's Putin and Turkey's Erdogan.

Have We Become "Unwitting Victims of the Darkness"?

Winston Churchill referred to the nerve-wracking years before World War II as "the gathering storm," which became the title of volume one of his magnificent history of the war. At that time, there was little brewing in the British Parliament or the

American Congress to raise hopes that courageous legislators would soon come up with plans to stop the menace posed by an aggressive Nazi leader. "The malice of the wicked," Churchill wrote, "was reinforced by the weakness of the virtuous. . . . They lived [from] one election to another. . . . The cheers of weak, well-meaning assemblies soon cease to echo, and their votes soon cease to count. Doom marches on."

Churchill thought of the years of the gathering storm as a transition from one era to another, from appeasement to war. On September 10, 1976, the British statesman, had he lived, would have been gratified to hear a sympathetic echo from the Supreme Court. Justice William O. Douglas tried to explain in a letter to the Washington State Bar Association that, when faced with a clear and present danger, people had only a limited amount of time to act. If they hesitated, for whatever reason, they might lose their chance, and the danger would soon be upon them. "As nightfall does not come at once," Douglas wrote, "neither does oppression. In both instances, there is a twilight when everything remains seemingly unchanged. And it is in such twilight that we all must be most aware of change in the air—however slight—lest we become unwitting victims of the darkness."

Douglas wrote this "in the twilight" letter following the American defeat in Vietnam, when people were disheartened by a government that did not seem to be working, a Central Intelligence Agency that seemed to have lost its soul, and a Congress that chose to look the other way. But in Douglas's view, the people, however disheartened, still had the chance to do something to head off the "darkness." Once in the darkness, it would have been too late to act. Douglas was pleading for a heightened sense of personal responsibility while there was still time.

Two Harvard professors have chosen this moment in American history to update Justice Douglas's warning. Steven Levitsky and Daniel Ziblatt, in a book somberly titled *How Democracies Die*, write that the days of military coups and fascist takeovers have passed and that "democratic backsliding begins at the ballot box." Politicians, already bitten by the authoritarian bug, are "legally" elected, the professors write, having run on promises to combat corruption, to improve the judicial system, and to clean up the rigged electoral process—in Trump's terminology, the "swamp in Washington." But once in power, either by design or accident, they slowly begin to accumulate more power by undermining competing positions of authority, such as the judiciary and the press.[2]

"Newspapers still publish," Levitsky and Ziblatt write, "but are bought off or bullied into self-censorship. Citizens continue to criticize the government but often find themselves facing tax or other legal troubles. This sows public confusion. People do not immediately realize what is happening. Many continue to believe they are living under a democracy."

Levitsky and Ziblatt are also describing a transition period, when action against creeping authoritarianism is still possible, shortly before the sweet light of freedom slips behind a cloud of indifference and democracy risks losing its vitality and relevance.

Talk to European diplomats, and you may hear some, less guarded than others, wonder aloud about whether we are all heading into another era of political oppression, when populists like Viktor Orban of Hungary, elected to office, then proclaim policies with rigid, nationalistic edges, curb the press and judiciary, protect their borders against African and Middle Eastern immigration, and then seriously consider withdrawing from pan-European institutions so honored until recently.

One also hears these same anguished worries from Japanese, Korean, and Australian diplomats. Often, in their comments, Trump is highlighted as one of the main reasons for their concerns. He is president of the United States, and as such, he automatically commands their attention, concern, and even fear.

When Trump pulled the United States out of the Iran nuclear deal in May 2018, German chancellor Angela Merkel described the president's decision as creating a "real crisis" in the global order. European Council president Donald Tusk was undiplomatically blunt in his assessment. *Washington Post* columnist David Ignatius reported that, in a tweet, Tusk fumed that "looking at the latest decision of [Trump] someone could even think: with friends like that, who needs enemies . . . thanks to him, we got rid of all illusions."

It is not only these foreign leaders and diplomats who worry that Trump may be splintering the Atlantic Alliance and bringing the United States closer to a form of authoritarianism. Former president Barack Obama shares the same fears, though he rarely expresses them in public. However, in December 2017, at the Economic Club of Chicago, he made it very plain that, in his view, the world now teeters on the brink of chaos; and while there is still time, he urged everyone to do something. "You have to tend to this garden of democracy," he said in a very sober tone of voice. "Otherwise things can fall apart fairly quickly. And we have seen societies where that happens." Obama clearly was thinking about pre–World War II Germany, Austria, and other countries in Western and Central Europe, where even sophisticated people thought everything was fine, until everything collapsed. "Presume there was a ballroom . . . in Vienna in the late 1920s or '30s that looked and seemed as if it, filled with the music and art and literature that was emerging," he went on, "would continue into perpetuity. And then 60 million people died. An entire world was plunged into chaos."

Not just Obama but many others as well are deeply concerned that Trump may be willing to do whatever is necessary to rally public support for himself, even if that means leading the world into a "wag the dog" war that would divert attention from his own failings and legal troubles.

Echoing the Obama message is former secretary of state Madeleine Albright. In her recent book, *Fascism: A Warning*, she sounds the alarm about the recent rise of populist authoritarianism. She points to Benito Mussolini, who screamed about "breaking the backs of the democrats," and Adolf Hitler, who "lied incessantly about himself and his enemies" and then started a war of aggression that led to tens of millions of deaths. Albright left the clear impression that when she wrote about the twentieth-century fascists, she was actually worrying about a twenty-first-century American demagogue.

Trump, as president, has already shown that he has little patience for the details of governing, and he certainly lacks an ideological vision or roadmap defining his authoritarian policies. He is no Mussolini or Hitler, but he is drawn toward government as a triumphant spectacle in his honor, with him on a Pennsylvania Avenue grandstand saluting troops and tanks parading before him. If they were returning from a war, the spectacle would be more dramatic. Trump thinks of all aspects of his presidency as a TV show, and he is again acting like the host, more feared than adored, who can fire anyone and even set the world ablaze. If, in this way, Trump has robbed the presidency of its former gravitas, its ability, almost magically, to inspire "new frontiers" of freedom and democracy, he offers no apologies, nor does he seem to recognize what he has done.

Trump has left many Americans in a political twilight zone between the democracy they have grown up to admire and the authoritarianism they fear may be just over the near horizon. If our fears prove to be unwarranted, then there will be plenty of time and space for general rejoicing. But if they prove to be prescient, there is still time to avoid becoming, in Justice Douglas's words, the "unwitting victims of the darkness."

Uncertainty, a Trump Legacy

Under President Trump, Americans have gotten used to living with deliberate uncertainty. "What has he done now?" is a question many ask as they turn on the evening or morning newscasts or scan the internet's headlines, and everyone knows who "he" is. They are not sure whether they will be greeted by news of another outrageous tweet, another scandal, another presidential promise of jobs, more jobs and even more jobs—in other words, prosperity of epic proportions, a stock market shooting through the roof, bonuses everywhere. There are also investigations into possible collusion among Trump, his people, and the Russians—all of it clouded by worries of war, stumbled into or deliberately promoted, or by twitching anxieties about another cataclysmic economic downturn. With Trump, we live in a fool's paradise, or one best defined by former secretary of defense Donald Rumsfeld's "known knowns, known unknowns and unknown unknowns." Trump comprises all the "knowns" and "unknowns" of modern American politics.

Through all the unknowns of the past, we have learned to depend on two institutions of American democracy to save us from a presidential swing toward authoritarianism: the judicial system and the press. Though it also would be reassuring to be able to depend on the elected representatives of the people, they are not at the moment the most reliable legislators on Earth, more absorbed with short-term political gain than with the longer-term interests of the country. Consider the comment of Senate Majority Leader Mitch McConnell: he defined 2017 as "the best year on all fronts," presumably based on the late December 2017 passage of a tax cut bill that rewarded Republican deep-pocket donors at the cost of sending the nation into a deeper long-term debt. If 2017 can be judged "the best year on all fronts," then the Republican Party has truly lost its way, abandoning principle to gushing obsequiousness before Trump, for whom praise of his "genius" has become the coin of the realm, certainly for Republican legislators, who bow on one knee before a Trumpian image of infallibility.

They, like everyone else, have also heard stories about whether Trump is "fit" to be president. Floating in the Washington ether is speculation, informed and often uninformed, that Trump suffers from a "malignant narcissism," a psychological ailment that impedes his ability to reach rational decisions. Twenty-seven psychiatrists and mental health professionals contributed articles to a book titled *The Dangerous Case of Donald Trump*, arguing that it was their professional responsibility, their "duty to warn" the nation of the dangers inherent in a Trump-led America. None of the authors had treated Trump. None knew him professionally, but all felt the urgent need to speak up—and they did.[3]

Almost as though in answer to the twenty-seven psychiatrists, a White House doctor examined Trump and then told reporters the president was in excellent health, having passed, in addition to everything else, a mental test that proved, he said, that Trump was fully capable of doing his job. Trump later nominated that doctor—a Navy admiral with little administrative experience—to head the huge Veterans Affairs Department. The admiral ultimately withdrew in the face of sustained criticisms about his personal behavior and workplace demeanor.

One Republican-turned-TV host and critic, Joe Scarborough, made headlines by reporting that a couple of the president's friends said that Trump was suffering from "early-stage dementia." On air, Scarborough added, "He repeats the same stories over and over again. His father had [the same ailment]. And it's getting worse, and not a single person who works for him doesn't know he has early signs of dementia." Scarborough tried to add the "dementia" angle to one of his weekly *Washington Post* columns, but editorial page editor Fred Hiatt x'ed it out, saying his source was not a "medical professional." Most editors would agree with Hiatt.

Trump can be unfit for the presidency without being mentally ill. Until it could be demonstrated, by medical test or professional diagnosis, that Trump was mentally ill, it would be inappropriate for journalists to state that he was mentally ill. It was, though, perfectly appropriate for a journalist, like any other citizen, to observe Trump at work and, after a while, conclude that he was unfit to be president.

"Only a Free and Unreserved Press"

Putting aside congressional hearings, special counsel investigations, and the November 2018 elections, it is left to two basic institutions of American democracy to confront the challenges posed by President Trump and his administration and, if possible, to save the nation: first, the judiciary, with its rulings, and second, the press, with its reporting. Without both of them doing their jobs, our democracy could be in serious peril. Up to this time, Trump has continued to belittle the judiciary, lambasting the "so-called judges" and even top Justice Department officials he has appointed. Each day he demeans the press, routinely accusing it of promulgating "fake news," especially when it is critical of him.

Edward R. Murrow always believed that "America" could best be defined as the nation with an independent judiciary and a fearless, free press. The two, in his mind, were intimately woven into a single fabric called "America." Trump has provided us with many reasons to be concerned about the continuing growth and vitality of "America," but I remain an optimist. Though often challenged, our democratic traditions have remained strong. And, Trump, though crafty, is really old-fashioned, his message tattered, and his personality an almost daily embarrassment to the nation he, as president, represents. He is damaged goods, and he will be replaced, the sooner the better, but only, one hopes, by legal means.

As a journalist and teacher for more than sixty years, I am aware of the manifold shortcomings of the press, which too often focuses on trivialities and in many respects has come to reflect, even amplify, the deep partisanship of the nation. But I am also proud of its role as a messenger of truth and a beacon of hope, wherever in the world freedom beckons. I remain convinced that a free press is the best guarantor of a free society. One is indissolubly linked to the other. James Madison, a founding father, understood better than most the value and importance of a free press. "To the press alone," he wrote, "checkered as it is with abuse, the world is indebted for all the triumphs which have been gained by reason and humanity over error and oppression."

Supreme Court Justice Hugo Black, who earlier in his

career was associated with the Ku Klux Klan but who saw the light and then served with distinction on the bench, defended First Amendment freedoms as fundamental to democracy. I have no doubt that, if he had met Trump, he would, without hesitation, have spoken truth to power. He would have stressed that the press existed not to flatter a president but to serve the public. And he would have explained why, as he did in the landmark Pentagon Papers case.

"In the First Amendment," Black said, "the Founding Fathers gave the free press the protection it must have to fulfill its essential role in our democracy." Then a pause for the key sentence. "The press was to serve the governed, not the governors." Then his concluding thought. "The press was protected so that it could bare the secrets of government and inform the people. Only a free and unrestrained press can effectively expose deception in government."

If President Trump is currently responsible for "deception in government," which is undeniably true, then both the deception and the deceiver must be exposed, and that is the job of the press. Why? Because, more than anything else, that is its "essential role in our democracy."

And so, with all due respect to the office you hold, Mr. President, the "enemy of the people" is not the press. It is you.

Notes

Chapter One

1. "President Trump Has Made 3,001 False or Misleading Claims So Far," *Washington Post*, April 30, 2018 (https://www.washingtonpost.com/graphics/politics/trump-claims-database/?utm_term=.aofec c871770).

2. David Leonhardt and Stuart A. Thompson, "Trump's Lies," *New York Times*, December 14, 2017 (https://www.nytimes.com/interactive/2017/06/23/opinion/trumps-lies.html).

3. Philip Bump, "Here Are All the Times We're Pretty Sure That Trump Was Watching Fox News as President," *Washington Post*, November 29, 2017 (https://www.washingtonpost.com/news/politics/wp/2017/11/29/here-are-all-the-times-were-pretty-sure-that-trump-was-watching-fox-news-as-president/?utm_term=.f3fd9e3bc494).

4. John Hayward, "Pat Caddell on 'Cooked' Reuters Poll: 'Never in My Life Have I Seen a News Organization Do Something So Dishonest,'" *Breitbart*, August 1, 2016 (www.breitbart.com/radio/2016/08/01/pat-caddell-on-cooked-reuters-poll-never-in-my-life-have-i-seen-a-news-organization-do-something-so-dishonest/).

5. Patrick Caddell, "Mainstream Media Is Threatening Our Country's Future," *Fox News Opinion*, September 29, 2012 (www

.foxnews.com/opinion/2012/09/29/mainstream-media-threatening-our-country-future.html).

6. *Tyndall Report*, "2016 Year in Review" (http://tyndallreport.com/yearinreview2016/).

7. Fox News, "The Media's Reputation Takes Another Hit," June 30, 2017 (www.foxnews.com/transcript/2017/06/30/medias-reputation-takes-another-hit.html).

8. Colum Lynch and Robbie Gramer, "Trump Appointee Compiles Loyalty List of U.S. Employees at U.N., State," *Foreign Policy*, June 13, 2018.

Chapter Two

1. "Khrushchev's Secret Speech, 'On the Cult of Personality and Its Consequences,' Delivered at the Twentieth Party Congress of the Communist Party of the Soviet Union," Wilson Center Digital Archive (http://digitalarchive.wilsoncenter.org/document/115995).

Chapter Three

1. Brian Stelter, "After Meeting with North Korean Dictator, Trump Calls Press America's 'Biggest Enemy,'" *CNN Money*, June 13, 2018.

2. Peter Beinart, "The New McCarthyism of Donald Trump," *The Atlantic*, July 21, 2015 (https://www.theatlantic.com/politics/archive/2015/07/donald-trump-joseph-mccarthy/399056/).

3. James Risen and Tom Risen, "Donald Trump Does His Best Joe McCarthy Impression," *New York Times*, June 22, 2017 (https://www.nytimes.com/2017/06/22/opinion/sunday/donald-trump-joseph-mccarthy-west-virginia.html).

4. Richard Cohen, "Trump Is a Modern-Day McCarthy," *Washington Post*, February 5, 2018 (https://www.washingtonpost.com/opinions/trump-is-a-modern-day-mccarthy/2018/02/05/7805dfac-0aa2-11e8-8b0d-891602206fbz_story.html?utm_term=.5defefd60524).

5. Elaine Kamarck, "Will the Trump Presidency Turn Out to Be Watergate, McCarthyism or Something Else Entirely?," Brookings, February 16, 2018 (https://www.brookings.edu/blog/fixgov/2018/02/16/watergate-mccarthyism-or-something-else-entirely/).

Chapter Four

1. "Excerpts from McCarthy's Speech to the Ohio Country Republican Women's Club," February 9, 1950, Ohio County Public Library (http://www.ohiocountylibrary.org/wheeling-history/5655#speech).

2. David Halberstam, *The Fifties* (New York: Random House, 1993), p. 55.

Chapter Five

1. "Declaration of Conscience," Statement of Senator Margaret Chase Smith, June 1, 1950, Margaret Chase Smith Library (https://web.archive.org/web/20150214191436/http://www.mcslibrary.org:80/program/library/declaration.htm).

Chapter Six

1. Jon Meacham, "Donald Trump and the Limits of the Reality TV President," *New York Times*, December 29, 2017 (https://www.nytimes.com/2017/12/29/opinion/donald-trump-reality-tv.html).

Chapter Eight

1. Starting in 1957, when I joined CBS, I wrote such commentaries for Murrow about developments in the communist world. The first was a Moscow visit by Egypt's Gamal Abdel Nasser. "What does this mean?," Murrow wanted to know. "Why is it so important?"

2. "A Report on Senator Joseph R. McCarthy," *See It Now*, March 9, 1954 (https://www.youtube.com/watch?v=-YOIueFbG4g).

Chapter Nine

1. "'You're Fake News!' The 2017 Poynter Media Trust Survey," Poynter Journalism Ethics Summit, December 4, 2017 (https://poyntercdn.blob.core.windows.net/files/PoynterMediaTrustSurvey2017.pdf).

2. Sara Fischer, "92% of Republicans Think Media Intentionally Reports Fake News," *Axios*, June 27, 2018.

3. Steven Shepard, "Poll: 46 percent Think Media Make Up Stories about Trump," *Politico*, October 18, 2017 (https://www.politico.com/story/2017/10/18/trump-media-fake-news-poll-243884).

4. Mike Allen, "1 Big Thing: Trump's Media Manipulation Machine," *Axios*, December 1, 2017 (https://www.axios.com/news letters/axios-am-679e449b-0057-41a9-b540-74cfa6d2fe68.html).

Chapter Ten

1. Carlos Lozada, "The Presidency Survived the Watergate, Iran-Contra and Clinton Scandals. Trump Will Exact a Higher Toll," *Washington Post*, December 21, 2007 (https://www.washing tonpost.com/news/book-party/wp/2017/12/21/the-presidency-sur vived-the-watergate-iran-contra-and-clinton-scandals-trump-will-exact-a-higher-toll/?noredirect=on&utm_term=.58bc56ef2f10).

2. Steven Levitsky and Daniel Ziblatt, *How Democracies Die* (New York: Penguin Random House, 2018).

3. Bandy X. Lee and others, *The Dangerous Case of Donald Trump: 27 Psychiatrists and Mental Health Experts Assess a President* (New York: St. Martin's Press, 2017).

Index